The

# London
## SHOPPING COMPANION

*Also available from Cumberland House*

# THE PARIS SHOPPING COMPANION
### SUSAN SWIRE WINKLER

The

# London

## SHOPPING COMPANION

## Nicki Pendleton Wood

CUMBERLAND HOUSE
NASHVILLE, TENNESSEE

Published by
CUMBERLAND HOUSE PUBLISHING, INC.
431 Harding Industrial Drive
Nashville, Tennessee 37211

Copyright © 2004 by Nicki Pendleton Wood

Cover design by Jules Rules, Nashville, Tennessee.

ISBN 1-58182-383-5

*Printed in the United States of America.*

1 2 3 4 5 6 7 8 9 10—07 06 05 04

To Eloise,

my London shopping companion,

and for England,

a nation of exceptional shopkeepers

# CONTENTS

# ACKNOWLEDGMENTS

Thanks are in order for those friends on both sides of the ocean who have cheerfully discussed their shopping habits with me, shopped with me, read draft pages, offered suggestions, provided childcare, and helped in so many other ways as this project took shape.

Thanks to Allison Blasch, Alison Bowery, and supershoppers Ashley C. Levi and Barrie Caldwell, Lyn Dean, Cathy Hardy, Melissa McPartland, Connally Davies Penley, Jill Pigott, Ron Pitkin, Nettie Smith, Nicola von Schreiber, and Antonia Watkins.

Special thanks to the Lams family of Nashville and London—Peter, Tina, Alison, and Boris—for the use of their digs in Dulwich, and to Jim Leeson for putting us together.

And most of all, thanks to my husband, Tom, whose extraordinary research skills and critical eye were, and are, indispensable.

# INTRODUCTION

When a British friend learned about this book, she commented, "When I go to the States, I wonder why anyone would shop in England when they could shop in America."

It's true, and it's not. London is undeniably expensive for everyday shopping and ordinary expenditures such as meals and transportation.

That said, much of Europe and Asia go to London to shop. Why? Because the selection and quality and range are unparalleled in most cities. You'll find more shops selling more things of better quality in more styles and varieties than just about anywhere else in Europe. Add to that matchless cultural opportunities and excellent streetscape, and you have the formula for consummate tourist appeal.

London concentrates a critical mass of talent and money that makes for great shopping. Apparently it has always been so—in the first century, Tacitus noted that London was "the chief residence of merchants" and "a great mart of trade and commerce." Talk about a long tradition of shopping, and all because . . .

More breeds more, and London just has more reasons to have more of everything. More royalty means more purveyors of world-class goods. More centers of learning mean more books. More brilliant designers mean more imaginative décor shops and ateliers. More museums and more imports mean more collectibles and antiquities. More fashion media mean more fashion. More superrich mean more shops competing for their discriminating patronage.

My shopping style tends to be targeted, but London browsing is hard to resist, knowing that around the corner could be a shop with the cutest-ever toys, the best-designed housewares, or must-have handbags. No matter what you're looking for, you won't be disappointed.

I've tried to include things not found in most U.S. cities—the handmade, the one-of-a-kind, the collectible, the unusual—the kinds of things that are so abundant in London.

I've also tried to include some shops that cater to hobbies and special interests. When I visit another country, I automatically go in search of handmade clothing, antique linens, old books, ephemera, musical recordings, products associated with cycling and cooking, fabric, needlework—these and other interests bring me to the door of a shop.

London is wonderful to visit with children, and I have offered a number of child-friendly options for shopping, eating, and recreation.

There's good shopping elsewhere, but London offers the exciting combination of exceptional shopping and outstanding cultural opportunities, all within several square miles. Wherever you might find yourself, there's something nearby to do or see, and I have included a few of these as notes titled "Culture Along the Way."

There's a wonderful British word, *moreish,* which denotes something so appealing it's hard to resist having more of it. Everything about London—from the meandering streets to the luxurious hotels, the public parks to the Underground, the museums to the people-watching—is moreish. The shopping may be the most moreish of all.

I believe every shop in this book offers something that will surprise, delight, inspire, enrich, or amuse you. London has thousands of wonderful stores, so if you think I've missed something special, or if you find that some of the following information has changed, please let me know. *The London Shopping Companion* will be updated periodically. Just send a note with your comments and all information to Nicki Pendleton Wood, c/o Cumberland House Publishing, 431 Harding Industrial Drive, Nashville, TN 37211.

# ABOUT SHOPPING IN LONDON

## WHEN TO GO

London is a pleasure to visit in all but the deep winter months. You can be reasonably assured of pleasant temperatures from mid-March to November, and of reliably dry weather from May to October. Visitors serious about shopping for bargains may wish to be in London during the annual sales in January and July.

## FINANCIAL MATTERS

Purchases made with credit cards receive the best exchange rate, something close to the interbank rate—but often there is a hidden fee rolled into the conversion figure that will appear on your statement. For security and convenience, you may wish to take along some traveler's checks denominated in pounds. ATM withdrawals are convenient and offer a good rate of exchange, though your home bank might tack on a charge.

### About British Prices

If you want to have a great shopping experience, you must first of all pledge not to buy American products in England. They are far more expensive than in the States. You'll find with brands or shops such as Nine West, Nike, Gap, Talbot's, Ralph Lauren, even Starbucks, that the figure on the price tag is the same as in the States, say, "68" for a pair of shoes. But that figure is in pounds, and when the pound is trading at $1.60, that item costs 60 percent more than it would in the States. Therefore, that £68 pair of shoes actually costs about $109. That's a midpriced pair of shoes in England, but a much finer pair in America.

Similarly, you should avoid buying imported products in England that are available in America. Shopping in a high-rent district such as London, combined with the 17.5 percent Value Added Tax (VAT), means that a clever T-shirt, Swatch watch, kilt, or pair of sunglasses will cost much more than in most U.S. cities of any size. Oxford and Regent Streets are not given expansive treatment here because of this.

I have included some establishments whose products have limited distribution in the United States. Sometimes such goods cost more in the States, and sometimes they cost less, so check prices before you buy in London.

A price range is given for each store, representing what you could expect to spend on a typical visit, from inexpensive ($—less than £100) to very expensive ($$$$—more than £2,000).

## Reclaiming Tax

Under a program called the Retail Export Scheme, you can reclaim the 17.5 percent Value Added Tax that is included in the price of goods sold in Britain. Retailers are not required to participate in this program, so ask before you drop a bundle. Though the law states that you can reclaim VAT on any purchase of more than £50, some stores have higher minimums.

The VAT refund system works in one of three ways:

1. Some merchants will sell an item tax-free if you can prove you are taking the item out of the European Union (EU) within three months from the end of the month in which it is purchased. (These stores often have a special sticker in the shop window that reads "Tax-Free Shopping.")

2. In other stores, you pay the tax but receive special VAT refund forms (or a special cash register receipt) at the time of purchase. The retailer should fill out his or her portion of the form, and you'll fill out the rest before you leave the country. Show your purchases and paperwork to Customs as you leave England (or the European Union) and claim your refund at a special desk located in most airports. (There is a refund desk at London Heathrow.) Expect to pay a commission of around £5 for your instant refund.

   A company called Global Refund (www.globalrefund.com) has an office at the Easy Internet Café, 358 Oxford Street, where you can collect your refund.

3. You can also receive a refund check by mail or as a credit to your credit card account. You should have received an envelope from the retailer along with your forms. Show the purchases and forms to Customs, then enclose the forms in the

envelope and deposit it in the special drop-box near the customs area at the airport. (These drop-boxes are also on cruise ships, should you leave England that way.) Receiving a refund by mail or as a credit to your credit card account takes about three months.

If you are traveling to other EU countries before you return to the United States, you must still show your goods and paperwork to Customs.

VAT on hotel accommodations, meals, and other services is not reclaimable. Some products also are not eligible for VAT reclaim: certain consumable items (food, perfume), mail-order items, cars, sailboats, and unmounted gemstones. There are also special rules for certain travelers, such as students and those with temporary British postings. Check Her Majesty's Customs and Excise page for these special rules at www.hmce.gov.uk. Click on "VAT refunds for visitors."

# TRANSPORTATION

Walking in pedestrian-friendly central London is part of the experience, but distances can mount if you're doing extensive shopping. Wear comfortable shoes.

The London Underground subway system, popularly called "the Tube," is famously simple to use and serves most of central London quite well. Single tickets are about £1.60 for adults, or 60 pence for children. A carnet (a pack of ten tickets) is a much better buy, offering ten tickets for a total of just £11.50 (adult). The tickets are good for twelve months. Travelcards, good on travel by suburban rail, underground, and bus for an entire day or longer periods, are often the best deal available.

London Transport buses go to areas between Tube stops, or off the beaten path, and are similarly straightforward—easy-to-read timetables are posted at each bus stop. All buses now require payment in advance of your ride, with ticket machines situated next to most stops. If your wanderings are going to take you into the more spread-out and residential areas south of the river Thames (not a hotbed of great shopping, and not covered here), you will probably need to get around in part by bus. I have noted in certain chapters which buses are particularly useful.

Taxis are expensive but convenient, though you may have trouble hailing one during rush hour or sudden downpours.

Should you be considering car rental, note that there now is a £5 daily "congestion charge" for driving in central London, though this may be covered in your rental fee. The charge has considerably diminished the volume of traffic, but you'll still have plenty of difficult urban navigation ahead, namely, closed and one-way streets, a jungle of signs, and infernally narrow lanes. Parking is scarce and expensive, though the larger department stores (Harrods, Selfridge's) have parking garages.

# NAVIGATION

You will need a copy of *London A to Z* (ask for an "A to Zed") to get the most from shopping excursions. Part of London's charm is its higgledy-piggledy street plan, but it can be exasperating, too. So use your *A to Z* with pride. Spiral-bound versions of the book are on sale at newsstands in and around all rail stations. You can resort to asking directions if necessary, but it's said that every fourth person on London's streets on any given day is an out-of-towner, so you may or may not be successful.

When you're heading for a particular retailer, be sure to note the full name of the street. London's streets are maddeningly named. Sometimes every street for blocks around will bear the same name, but with a different designation (e.g., Montpelier Square, Montpelier Row, Montpelier Terrace, and Montpelier Mews).

Conversely, streets with nearly identical names can appear several blocks apart or in adjacent parts of town: Bury Walk is in Chelsea, Bury Place is in Bloomsbury, and Bury Street is in St. James. Duke of York Street is in St. James, but Duke of York Square is off Kings Road. To avoid confusion, addresses in this book include a partial postal code, as well as the nearest Tube stop.

# LONDON HOTELS

Even the British say it—hotel accommodations in England are expensive for what you get. And London hotels are the extreme, offering small rooms for lots of money. A $150 (£95) single room in a mid-grade central London hotel is considered a fantastic value, while a family room in such a hotel would go for about $350 (£225).

Why do Brits and others put up with these prices? Because if you find a less expensive room, it's likely to be minuscule, with grim décor and desperately cheap furnishings, in an establishment with no lobby and iron bars around the reception desk.

At the $200 (£125) per night level, you begin to get a glimmer of the décor and services you'd expect in a midrange U.S. hotel. If you want real charm, luxury, and service, you can expect the rates to start at about $350 (£225) per night.

With that in mind, the hotels selected for this book offer some value for your money, whether that value is monetary, a dash of extra charm or style, a great location, or superb amenities for the price. I have made a special effort to include places that offer reasonably priced family accommodations.

If you're serious about saving money and don't mind an extra Tube stop or two, you might look for lodging in the Bayswater and Pimlico areas. Rooms here are often priced lower than central London rooms, while the locations are still quite near desirable tourist and shopping destinations.

Three hotel chains that consistently offer moderately priced rooms in London are Thistle, Best Western, and Comfort Inn/Country Inn & Suites, and all have several properties around the city. The rooms won't have the charm and individuality of an independently owned property, but you will find a room for a price that won't break the bank.

## PREVIEWING A SHOP

Many London shops have excellent websites that let you view the merchandise or even take a virtual tour of the store. These are indicated in the listings.

A site that lets you see a full streetscape including the shop you want to visit is www.streetsensation.co.uk. The site also includes maps, so you get a feel for where a shop is in relation to various landmarks. It is updated frequently with closures and openings. If you're a precision shopper, you'll get much out of this site.

### Shop Closures

Shops are born and die more frequently in London than in U.S. cities. The economic climate of the past several years has only accelerated this tendency. Stores with several branches around the city may opt to close underperforming units. So if you are specifically planning a shopping trip around a particular branch, telephone first to establish that it is still operating.

## TELEPHONE

London telephone numbers have undergone three changes of area code in the past twenty years, the latest resulting in most 0171 numbers being changed to 0207 and 0181 numbers to 0208. If you are in possession of an old London telephone number, you can verify it at www.yell.com, the British online yellow pages.

The phone numbers in this book are generally shown as a four-digit code (usually 0207) followed by a seven-digit number, to make them more recognizable to those familiar with U.S.-style telephone numbers.

To call from within England, dial the phone numbers as written. When calling a London establishment from outside England, use the international access number (011), the country code (44), and omit the initial zero from the area code.

The **London**

SHOPPING COMPANION

# MAYFAIR/ST. JAMES

$\mathcal{M}$AYFAIR/ST. JAMES IS THE premier shopping district in London. It's so large and abundant in shopping that I've divided it into two areas. St. James is the area along and south of Piccadilly, including Jermyn and St. James Streets. Mayfair, where a rowdy fair was held each May long ago, is the area north of Piccadilly, including Bond Street, Savile Row, Conduit Street, and South Molton.

## WHERE TO STAY

PARK LANE is the premier hotel address in this part of London, but I find the hotels here out of my price range and an uncomfortable walking distance from Knightsbridge and the parts of Mayfair and St. James that I really want to visit. Still, if your taste runs to four- and five-star luxury right on Hyde Park, then this is the home base you're looking for. The Metropolitan (the restaurant Nobu is here), Dorchester, London Hilton, Grosvenor House, and Inter-Continental are some of the top names in this area.

## Westbury Hotel

The Westbury is the only hotel on Bond Street in the very heart of Mayfair, so it's ideally situated for shopping. There are 247 rooms, of which 25 are suites, and some rooms have balconies overlooking the street. The rooms aren't individually decorated but are attractive enough. All but the priciest rooms are small by U.S. standards but average for London. Amenities include a

ADDRESS
Bond Street
(entrance on Conduit Street)
W1S

PHONE
0207 629 7755

WEBSITE
www.westburymayfair.com

E-MAIL
reservations@westburymayfair.com

terrific concierge, dial-up Internet service (with both U.S. and British modem jacks), pay-per-view movies, and a fitness center with plenty of equipment. The breakfast room is especially pretty. For chilly days, there's a fireplace in the restaurant, which serves good, traditional English food and some new Euro dishes. Scary fact: The hotel's Polo Lounge bar in London is identical to the one in the now-closed New York West-bury, so if you are a continental traveler, you can sit at the bar and not know from the surroundings which city you are in.

Shoppers get special treatment at the Westbury. The hotel has an arrangement with about twenty local mer-chants that gives a 10 percent discount to people who are staying at the Westbury. Participating shops include Ungaro, Moschino, Aquascutum, Escada, Marina Rinaldi, Cerruti 1881, Lanvin, and DKNY.

Published, or "rack," rates for single rooms start at £240, suites from £350, not including VAT. But the Westbury is working hard to be competitive, so check with them before you book—good discounts may be available.

## Fleming's Mayfair Hotel

ADDRESS
Half Moon Street
W1J

PHONE
0207 493 2088

WEBSITE
www.flemings-mayfair.co.uk

Fleming's is a luxury 121-room hotel, with all that label entails, but at a price considered affordable for this part of London. A lovely Georgian townhouse on a quiet street that runs into Curzon near Shepherd's Market (*see page 44*), Fleming's features clubby, comfy sitting rooms, an all-knowing concierge, a restaurant with fixed-price lunch and dinner menus, newspapers, bathrobes, and all the goodies you expect.

At this writing, Fleming's has overhauled about a third of its guest rooms (all rooms are air-conditioned). Those that have been updated are sleek and modern, with flat-screen TV/DVD/computers; the general English country-house flounce of the older rooms is looking a little dated.

Single rooms are available from £169 (but I got one for half that price, so check before you go), doubles from £199 (not including VAT), updated rooms from £220. The website has detailed notes on the facility and photos of the common rooms and bedrooms.

The **Hilton Green Park Hotel,** just across Half Moon Street, offers upscale chain lodging in a similar price bracket. It also was undergoing a refurb in late 2003. (Phone: 020 7629 7522; website: www.hilton.com)

## Duke's Hotel

Duke's is an elegant townhouse that surrounds a lovely, gas-lit courtyard off a narrow street. The eighty-nine air-conditioned rooms are beautifully, even sumptuously, decorated, with updated marble baths. Luxurious, thoughtful touches include satellite TV, a jogging guide to the area, voice mail, and two phones in each room. There is twenty-four-hour room service, a well-equipped fitness center, a bar, a private dining room, and a business center with broadband Internet access.

Singles are available from £195 plus VAT; junior suites from £295; suites from £350.

ADDRESS
St. James Place
SW1A
PHONE
0207 491 4840 (or use the toll-free U.S. number: 800-381-4702)
WEBSITE
www.dukeshotel.com

## MAYFAIR SHOPS

### 1   Gray's Antique Market
*Antiques, Vintage Clothing, Jewelry, Collectibles, Coins, Boxes*

ADDRESS
58 Davies
W1K
PHONE
0207 629 7034
HOURS
Mon.–Fri. 10:00 a.m.–6:00 p.m.

Located just outside the Bond Street Tube station, this market comprises two buildings: Gray's, nearer the Tube station; and Gray's Mews, several doors down.

Gray's has exceptionally good jewelry stalls, many of which sell wares of quality far above the bric-a-brac jewelry usually found in markets. There are acres of silver and gold, much antique jewelry, and many high-end pre-owned pieces.

## ALONG SOUTH MOLTON

Some of the shops on South Molton change hands fairly often, but whatever moves in is usually fun. Try TURQUOISE, 7 South Molton Lane, if you want to dress like a rock star but just can't seem to find anything to your taste. Funky, flouncy, dramatic clothes with loads of details that shout, "Look at me!"

FRENCH FOR LESS offers Parisian looks at affordable prices: a long sweater coat for £149, knit trousers for £99, a knit tunic for £99, and a suit jacket for £99 and trousers for £49.

At the moment, CALVIN KLEIN'S underwear shop is also on South Molton Lane.

Besides plenty of gold, silver, and rings, expect to find Victorian jet jewelry, pearls of every size, and masses of cameos. Inspect the silver specialists' stalls for semi-affordable silver trinkets. There are also stalls of fine old linens, books, and ephemera.

The stall of JOHN JOSEPH (stands 345–346) is notable for its exceptional Victorian and Edwardian jewelry. Get a mouthwatering preview of his bijoux offerings at www.john-joseph.co.uk (phone: 0207 629 1140).

SYLVIE SPECTRUM, in stand 372, has perhaps the best prices in Gray's on modest pieces of gold and precious-stone jewelry.

Gray's Mews is the more interesting building—it has a little stream with ponds running through the ground floor that should entertain children while you shop for antique toys at stand B25, fabulous vintage clothing at stands 1 through 7, ancient coins at stand L17, or Limoges and other collectible boxes at L15 (www.michaelsboxes.com).

The Gray's Mews building has a 1950s-style diner called the Victory Café on the ground floor. The menu is modest—all-day breakfast, sandwiches, quiche—but everything, including the fries, is fresh and handmade (*see page 43 for a full description*).

## 2   Brown's

*Designer Fashion*

Some days, it looks as though everyone in this part of London shops at Brown's, and that's because it's one of the favorite, if most expensive, stores in town for designer fashion. An outfit from Brown's will be the most fashionable thing you'll ever own, and the staff is knowledgeable and helpful about putting together something smart. Shopping here is a survey of what's happening in European (and Australasian) fashion design—once you get past the sticker shock (£200 jeans, for instance). Brown's also represents many American designers, so shop carefully.

Next door is a Brown's home store, and BROWN'S FOCUS, a store for teens, is located across South Molton.

The Brown's sale shop, LABELS FOR LESS, is just down the street at 50 South Molton Lane. There you might find an Alexander McQueen pink blazer for £130, men's shirts for £20, a Brown's own-label leather coat for £175, or a Jil Sander jacket for £270.

ADDRESS
23–27 South Molton Lane
W1K (Bond Street Tube)

PHONE
0207 514 0000

HOURS
Mon.–Fri. 10:00 a.m.–6:30 p.m.
(open Thurs. until 7:00 p.m.)
$$$

BRANCH
KNIGHTSBRIDGE
6c Sloane Street
SW1 (Knightsbridge Tube)

PHONE
0207 514 0040

## 3   Butler & Wilson

*Costume Jewelry*

At Butler & Wilson you'll find gorgeous, often dramatic, costume jewelry that's hard to resist. The South Molton store (the flagship is in Fulham, southwest of the center) has a glass case of tiaras to swoon over and handbags so cute you'll be tempted despite their impracticality. All the jewelry is elaborate, ornate, dangly, complicated, and/or outrageous. A belt of shells and tassels goes for £98.

ADDRESS
20 South Molton Lane
W1

PHONE
0207 409 2955

HOURS
Mon.–Sat. 10:00 a.m.–6:00 p.m.
(open Thurs. until 7:00 p.m.); Sun.
12:00 p.m.–6:00 p.m.
$$

ADDRESS
21 South Molton Lane
WIK

PHONE
0207 629 6325

HOURS
Mon.–Fri. 10:00 a.m.–6:00 p.m.;
Sat. 10:00 a.m.–5:00 p.m.
$–$$$

## 4   Electrum Gallery

*Jewelry Gallery, Jewelry, Artisanal*

Electrum is a showroom for the weird, wonderful, and gorgeous jewelry offerings of around one hundred artists from all over the world. Strolling among the cases is a visual treat; your eyes move from something delicate to something bold, from something with a tribal look to something space age. Eccentricities are many, as are big and luxe pieces, but you'll undoubtedly fall in love with something. There are some quite expensive items here, but also some modestly priced. If you don't see exactly what you want, commissions can be arranged.

## South Molton Shopping Area

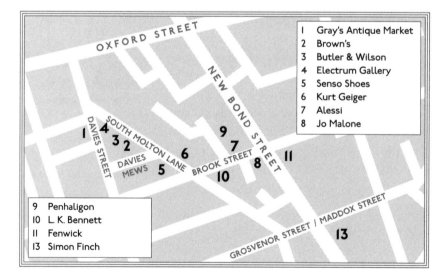

1   Gray's Antique Market
2   Brown's
3   Butler & Wilson
4   Electrum Gallery
5   Senso Shoes
6   Kurt Geiger
7   Alessi
8   Jo Malone

9   Penhaligon
10  L. K. Bennett
11  Fenwick
13  Simon Finch

## FRENCH CLOTHING FOR CHILDREN

Stylish French-made children's clothing often costs less in England than in the States, since the UK, being an EU country, has no tariff built into its prices. Also, children's clothing is not subject to the 17.5 percent VAT. Still, to get the best buys, be aware of the comparable U.S. prices before you shop.

South Molton has a PETIT BATEAU (children's clothing) and a TARTINE ET CHOCOLAT (children's clothing, baby gifts). Petit Bateau is best known for comfortable, well-designed cotton clothing that wears like iron and keeps its shape. Its T-shirts are so well-made and stylish that even small grownups wear them. They're inexpensive, too—a T-shirt that sells in New York for $30 is about £12 in London.

Tartine et Chocolat is ideal for pretty, sometimes extravagant, children's clothes and smart baby gifts. Well-designed diaper bags and handsome baby brush and bath sets make nice cadeaux.

BONPOINT (children's clothing, see page 70) has three London locations offering its well-designed togs: a newly opened Bond Street location, a Sloane Street shop, and a Westbourne Grove shop in Notting Hill. Prices are high but lower than in the States.

Also worth investigating are the lovely things at PETIT ANGE (children's clothing, see page 69).

## 5   Senso Shoes

*Women's Shoes*

After you see all the fashion-victim shoes in London's shoe shops, come to Senso for a more comfortable, but dead-stylish, approach to shoes. Senso commissions its own brand, Kim Meller, and carries the designs of Anna Sui and others.

ADDRESS
6 South Molton Lane
W1

PHONE
0207 499 9998

HOURS
Mon.–Sat. 10:00 a.m.–6:30 p.m. (open Thurs. until 7:00 p.m.); Sun. 1:00 p.m.–5:00 p.m.

$$

ADDRESS
65 South Molton Lane
W1

PHONE
0207 758 8025

HOURS
Mon.–Sat. 10:00 a.m.–7:00 p.m.;
Sun. 12:00 p.m.–6:00 p.m.
$–$$

BRANCH:
133 Kensington High Street
London
W8 (Kensington High Street Tube)

PHONE
0207 937 3716

## 6　Kurt Geiger

*Women's and Men's Shoes*

Another good shop for wearable, affordable shoes. This shop, Geiger's flagship, has very stylish women's and men's shoes at middling prices. Young, flexible feet can slip into something fun and funky for day or the strictly club-scene Gina shoes for nightlife. Working women will appreciate the lower-heeled pumps and handsome boots. The fresh, attractive KG brand is appealing, too. Sale prices are especially reasonable. You can get Geiger shoes at Selfridge's, Liberty, and Harrods as well. Geiger, like Harrods, is owned by the flamboyant Mohamed al-Fayed.

ADDRESS
22 Brook Street
W1A (Bond Street Tube)

PHONE
0207 518 9091

HOURS
Mon.–Sat. 10:30 a.m.–6:30 p.m.;
Sun. 1:00 p.m.–5:00 p.m.
$

## 7　Alessi

*Italian Household Designs, Kitchenware, Housewares*

Their world famous teapot is just one element of the Alessi tradition of high-design household items since the 1920s. Look for colorful plastic can openers (£26), calculators, soap dishes (£14), watches, corkscrews, clocks, dog bowls, and cookie boxes (£32). Phillippe Starck is one of their better-known designers, but the most famous is Michael Graves, whose work can now be seen at Target stores. The selection is large, so you're sure to find something you like, whether practical or whimsical. Good stop for gifts.

## Also on Brook Street:

8　**Jo Malone** (*fragrance, skin care; see page 67*)

9　**Penhaligon's** (*fragrance, shaving supplies; see page 77*)

10　**L. K. Bennett** (*women's clothing, women's shoes; see page 89*)

STROLL ALONG Bond Street, possibly the most designer-packed street in Europe, to ogle the world-class fashions, jewelry, and homewares at Miu Miu, Versace, Lanvin, Chanel, Bulgari, Nicole Farhi, Hermes, Mikimoto, Cartier, Frette, Armani, Ermenegildo Zegna, Furla, Anne Fontaine, Burberry, Donna Karan, Charles Jourdan, Ferragamo, Blumarine, Prada, and Alexander McQueen, plus dozens of others. This is the high-rent district, but the sales begin in January and July, when you just might find something fabulous at a reduced price.

## 11   Fenwick

*Department Store, Designer Fashion*

People are divided about Fenwick. Some say it's the best little department store around. Some feel it's a fairly average store with good designer departments. Both groups are right. This isn't the place to pop in for a pair of socks or a plain white blouse (try Peter Jones for that), but if you want to invest in a designer outfit and want plenty of choices, Fenwick is good. They have a vast selection of Annette Gortz's brilliant, handsome clothes, and an equally huge selection of Armani, Nicole Farhi, and Joseph for women. The men's department carries Paul Smith clothes, which manage to be simultaneously conventional and stylish. The top floor has designer youth and weekend looks.

Joe's restaurant on the second floor is always crowded, and Carluccio's in the basement is deservedly popular (*see page 42*). The bathrooms are ornate and lovely, and there's a big tray of fragrances to complete your toilette.

ADDRESS
63 New Bond Street
W1A

PHONE
0207 629 9161

HOURS
Mon.–Sat. 10:00 a.m.–6:30 p.m. (open Thurs. until 8:00 p.m.); closed Sun.
Website
www.fenwick.co.uk
(Check for any special offers or promotions before your visit.)
$$–$$$

## 12   Charbonnel et Walker

*Chocolates and Confections*

If your sugar level is dangerously low after a spell of shopping, pop into Charbonnel et Walker in the Royal Arcade, located off Bond Street, for a chocolate. Choose from traditional flavors or pick a champagne truffle, a chocolate-covered ginger marzipan, or a Scotch-and-praline chocolate.

ADDRESS
One Royal Arcade
28 Old Bond Street
W1

PHONE
0207 491 0939
$

ADDRESS
53 Maddox Street
WIS

PHONE
0207 499 0974

HOURS
Mon.–Fri. 10:00 a.m.–6:00 p.m.;
closed Sat.
$$–$$$$

BRANCH:
NOTTING HILL
61A Ledbury Road
Specializes in twentieth-century
collectible books.

## 13 Simon Finch
*Antique Books, Ephemera*

There are so many great antique book dealers in London, it's hard to know where to start. I love Simon Finch's unstuffy, relaxed atmosphere. This shop is one of two in London, the other being on Ledbury Road in Notting Hill (*see page 196*). Maddox Street carries pre-1850 books and specializes in English literature, human sciences, early printing, fine bindings, and science and medicine on five floors connected by a spiral staircase.

ADDRESS
15 Savile Row
WIS

PHONE
0207 734 5985
$$$$

## 14 Henry Poole
*Custom Tailor*

Henry Poole, established in 1806, is one of the oldest bespoke tailors on Savile Row. It's a fantastically interesting place to visit, both to see how the tailoring process works and to see the antiques and memorabilia.

Founder Henry Poole originally produced military uniforms then moved into livery and hunting pinks. The firm was court tailor to Emperor Napoleon III (Prince Louis Napoleon) and later to Queen Victoria's court. Along the way, Poole has made suits and livery for J. P. Morgan, Charles Dickens, and the Rothschilds. The firm still holds a royal warrant from Queen Elizabeth II for livery, one of several warrants lining the walls of the shop.

The shop houses two cabinets filled with fabulous things the tailors have made for dignitaries, such as Haile Selassie's epaulets, a garter robe that Churchill wore, and various other garments and finery.

Henry Poole, like many bespoke tailors, has preserved and displayed its ledgers from the nineteenth century.

Oh, and they make gorgeous suits from the finest fabrics. Unlike some custom tailors, Poole still does most of its work on the premises.

## 15   Ozwald Boateng

*Custom Tailor*

ADDRESS
9 Vigo Street
W1S

PHONE
0207 734 6868

HOURS
Mon.–Sat. 10:00 a.m.–6:00 p.m.
$$$$

If Henry Poole is the grand old man of Savile Row, Ozwald Boateng is one of the new guys in town, his shop having opened in the early 1990s. You've seen his suits in *Snatch, The Matrix Reloaded,* and on Pierce Brosnan in James Bond films. Boateng's choices of brilliant colors reflect his African Ashanti heritage, and his subtly stylish cuts mean his celebrity clientele runs to mostly show-business types. Nowadays, his suits begin at £2,200.

## 16   Marks Fine Antique Silver

*Fine Silver, Silver, Collectibles, Antiques*

ADDRESS
49 Curzon Street
W1

PHONE
0207 499 1788

HOURS
Mon.–Fri. 9:30 a.m.–6:00 p.m.;
Sat. 9:30 a.m.–5:00 p.m.

WEBSITE:
www.marksantiques.com
$$$$

Marks has been offering fine silver to the serious collector for forty years, first under the guidance of the founder, Albert Marks, and then his son, the current proprietor, Anthony Marks. Shortly before we stopped by, the firm sold a pair of Queen Anne wine coolers with David Willaume's maker's mark (1658–1741), which had lain for decades, forgotten by the owners, in a London bank vault. The price: £1 million.

Marks publishes a thick, hardbound catalog of its offerings about every eighteen months, which is a dazzling read worthy of coffee-table placement. Nearly life-size photos of sumptuous candelabra, bowls, champagne buckets, salt cellars, Russian lacquer boxes, and such from the finest workshops in Europe fill the pages. While most of the pieces are astronomically expensive, there are items priced around £300. If you're a serious silver buff, you'll meet your match in the highly knowledgeable staff at Marks. And if you are more interested in looking than acquiring, they're also very nice about that. Marks exhibits annually at New York's Armory Show and in Palm Beach. The shop has a branch outpost within the silver department of Harrods.

## A SHOPPER'S WALK THROUGH MAYFAIR

You can see many of the shops detailed here by taking the following route: Exit the Bond Street Tube station through the exit marked "Davies Street" (this will take a little searching) and you'll be on South Molton Lane, at the entrance to Gray's Antique Market. Slide through a little passage, and you'll be on South Molton Lane.

At the end of South Molton Lane, turn left, and you'll find Alessi a few doors down and Jo Malone across the street. At Alessi, look for the green and white flags of the Fenwick department store on New Bond Street. Walk down Bond to Sotheby's, then turn left onto Conduit Street. Walk along Conduit Street, then turn right on Savile Row. Savile Row runs into Piccadilly across from Fortnum & Mason, near the Royal Academy.

Or, from Savile Row, take a left onto a street called both Vigo and Burlington Gardens and pass through the Burlington Arcade.

## St. James Shopping Area

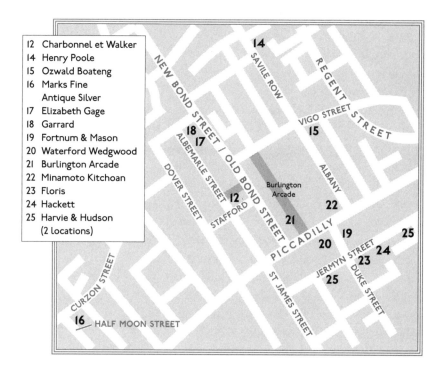

12 Charbonnel et Walker
14 Henry Poole
15 Ozwald Boateng
16 Marks Fine
   Antique Silver
17 Elizabeth Gage
18 Garrard
19 Fortnum & Mason
20 Waterford Wedgwood
21 Burlington Arcade
22 Minamoto Kitchoan
23 Floris
24 Hackett
25 Harvie & Hudson
   (2 locations)

## 17 Elizabeth Gage

*Fine Jewelry*

Jewelry designer Elizabeth Gage turns out bold, beautiful pieces of tasteful, up-to-date jewelry using large gems and ancient themes for impact. She shows her pieces in the States, usually Palm Beach, at least once a year. You can see a few of her pieces on the website.

ADDRESS
20 Albemarle Street
W1S

PHONE
0207 499 2879

HOURS
Mon.–Fri. 10:00 a.m.–5:30 p.m.

WEBSITE
www.whoswhoingoldandsilver.com
$$$–$$$$

## 18 Garrard

*Crown Jeweler, Jewelry*

Established in 1735, Garrard was named crown jeweler by Queen Victoria in 1843. More recently, Garrard has also begun reaching out to the world's "new royalty" by employing Jade Jagger as a designer of new jewelry lines that appeal to wealthy customers wanting some flash.

The result is that goods at the front and back of the store are wildly divergent. In the front are Jagger's jewel-encrusted pendants resembling automobile hood ornaments. You should decide for yourself whether she is earning her reported $700,000 annual salary. The crown jewel action is in the rear room, where several cases hold old-style massive pearl and gem necklaces more traditionally associated with the gem-wearing classes. It's like a free, private visit to the crown jewel exhibition, so it's worth ducking in here.

The upstairs is similarly split between ancient and modern aesthetics. Fine antique tea sets are displayed alongside 18-karat-gold pet jewelry and key chains bearing Garrard's emblem.

ADDRESS
24 Albemarle Street
W1S

PHONE
0870 871 8888

HOURS
Mon.–Fri. 10:00 a.m.–6:00 p.m.;
Sat. 10:00 a.m.–5:00 p.m.; closed
Sun.

$$$–$$$$

# ST. JAMES SHOPS

THE AREA south of Piccadilly is named for St. James Palace, the official residence of Prince Charles. The shops here were established to cater to royalty and their households.

ADDRESS
181 Piccadilly Street
W1 (Green Park Tube)

PHONE
0207 734 8040

HOURS
Mon.–Sat. 10:00 a.m.–6:30 p.m.;
Sun. (food hall and Patio restaurant
only) 12:00 p.m.–6:00 p.m.

WEBSITE
www.fortnumandmason.com
$–$$$

# 19 Fortnum & Mason

*Department Store*

At the top of the hour, gather with the crowd on Piccadilly to hear the whimsical old clock chime. Then nip inside to the food hall to be spoiled by the extraordinary array of teas, the incredible bakery, and the first-rate deli. Or have a meal at one of the restaurants. Be sure to note the gourmet Hershey's syrup and Skippy peanut butter among the other high-end victuals. Every American expat quickly learns what favorite grocery items are not sold in British supermarkets, and the truly homesick will pay a premium for a flavor of home: An ordinary package of Oreos at F&M sells for £6.

As well as luxury comestibles, there are plenty of small, affordable treats here. For instance, sample the taste of an English birthday with a prepackaged single-serving birthday cake.

On a nice day, pick up a sandwich and a serving of salad from the deli counter, a sweet or two from the bakery, and perhaps a bottle of wine, then take them down the street to Green Park. Rent a deck chair or sit on the soft grass and enjoy your lunch, accompanied by a bit of people-watching.

On the floors above and below the food hall are uncrowded departments of a very fine, traditional English department store. The lower ground floor is filled with gorgeous breakables and fancies for home and garden. The first floor has a small but excellent children's department and a selection of high-quality toys (no Power Rangers here). The women's department features grown-up and gorgeous clothes, dresses for weddings and garden parties, handsome suits (£650 is a typical price), and some very fetching hats, the kind worn at Ascot.

The gift department, next to menswear, and the next-door paper department have terrific inspirations for giving: expensive-looking executive desktop items (boxes, paperweights, globes) and gorgeous writing and wrapping papers.

## 20 Waterford Wedgwood
*Fine China, Collectibles, Crystal*

Here you'll find extensive offerings of the classic, luxurious tableware and barware you expect, plus some contemporary styles you'd never associate with these brands, along with jewelry items ideal for gifts. If traditional Wedgwood isn't for you, maybe you'll be inspired by the innovative Rosenthal designs, including Andy Warhol images of daisies, Beethoven, or Grace Kelly on porcelain (£12 for a mug, £60 for a dish, £175 for a large vase).

A Wedgwood jewelry piece would make an out-of-the-ordinary souvenir of your London visit. Many styles of pendants and earrings, cuff links, and tie clips are priced around £50. Here, too, you have a choice of traditional Wedgwood cameo designs or handsome, modern motifs.

ADDRESS
173 Piccadilly
W1

PHONE
0207 629 2614

HOURS
Mon.–Fri. 9:00 a.m.–6:00 p.m.;
Sat. 9:30 a.m.–6:00 p.m.
$–$$$

BRANCH:
158 Regent Street
PHONE
0207 734 7262

## 21 Burlington Arcade

Burlington Arcade (W1) is one of several arcades in this area good for a stroll to see what catches your fancy. Some of the highlights include:

- **Daniel Bexfield Antiques**—very fine silver and tempting silver trinkets.
- **N. Peale** has several of the storefronts in Burlington Arcade displaying fun, nontraditional cashmere styles in yummy colors.
- **Georgina von Etzdorf**'s scrumptious, sometimes indescribable, scarves, throws, and shawls in delicious colors and fabrics are favorites of well-dressed Londoners. The shop has a small selection of dresses and hand-painted bags. One season, the loveliest scarf was a delicate strand of fabric flowers like a lei. (Phone: 020 7409 7789; e-mail: gvelondon@ hotmail.com)

ADDRESS
44 Piccadilly
W1 (Green Park Tube)

PHONE
0207 437 3135

HOURS
10:00 a.m.–8:00 p.m. daily
$

## 22  Minamoto Kitchoan

*Japanese Confections*

You came to London for something different, right?
Well here's your place—a Japanese confectionery.
Fruits, nuts, bean paste, and rice are crafted into sweets
that resemble, or at least evoke, seasonal fruits, nuts, and
flowers. The sweets and the packaging are so delicate
and beautiful, you'll be tempted to buy a whole box.
The taste, though, may be a little foreign to Western
palates, so you might first sample what you're tempted
to buy (for £1 to £3 each). There's a New York store, in
case you get hooked.

ADDRESS
87 Jermyn Street
SW1 (Green Park Tube)

PHONE
0207 930 1300

HOURS
Mon.–Fri. 9:30 a.m.–6:00 p.m.;
Sat. 10 a.m.–6:00 p.m.

WEBSITE
www.florislondon.com
$–$$

## 23  Floris

*Fragrances*

There's no shortage of fragrance purveyors in London,
but for quality and exclusivity, Floris is arguably the best
(and my favorite). The shop was originally opened in
1730 by Juan Famenias Floris, from the Spanish isle of
Menorca, to sell handmade combs. He branched out
into fragrances, with which the shop is now most
strongly associated.

The fragrances are exceptionally pure, and a dose is
bracingly strong. Even a splash of eau de toilette lasts
for hours. The lavender is the finest you're likely ever to
encounter, a far cry from what passes for lavender scent
in most places. The unisex Santal is spicy; the Seringa a
light floral. They're all exquisite enough to make you
switch from other perfumes. There are four men's fragrances, all with a traditional, clean appeal, and shaving
supplies.

If you need more proof of the company's excellence,
Floris has two royal warrants: as perfumers to HM
Queen Elizabeth II and as manufacturers of toilet
preparations to HRH the Prince of Wales.

Prices are not especially high, given the quality. The lavender eau de toilette sells for £34 for 100 ml (about 3.25 ounces); bath oil for £16.50.

Unlike many of London's fragrance shops, there's only one location of Floris, though it is also available at Peter Jones department store (*see page 62*) and other London department stores. There's a small museum in back that showcases some of the company's packaging and products over the years, including a letter of thanks from Florence Nightingale for supplies of scent to spruce up her hospital. The staff are glad to show the room if you ask, and it's worth a visit.

## THE MEN'S ROOM

St. James, the nearest shopping district to Buckingham Palace, was developed to serve the kings and queens of England and their households. With the royals came the nobles, and around them grew a network of men's clubs. The menswear and other masculine industries of Savile Row and Jermyn Street developed to serve the royals and nobles.

Jermyn Street is where you'll find men's shirtmakers, a few tailors, and shoe stores. Shirtmakers include Thomas Pink, Coles of Jermyn Street, T. M. Lewin, and Turnbull & Asser. John Lobb shoes is here, too.

The area also offers manly pleasures and pastimes. Alfred Dunhill's flagship tobacco store, at the corner of Jermyn and Duke Streets, offers a big humidor of cigars, along with leather chairs in which to enjoy them. Pipe tobaccos are upstairs. Downstairs is the Dunhill museum, which has a fascinating collection of pipes, smoking gear, and store memorabilia. In the nearby Piccadilly Arcade is Astley's the Pipeseller, for expensive but distinctive pipes.

Cigarmaker Davidoff is at the corner of Jermyn and St. James. And for a cigar of Churchillian dimensions, visit James J. Fox & Robert Lewis, on St. James, where Winston Churchill bought his cigars. In the back room is a little museum of tobacco and historic memorabilia and (believe it or not) famous cigars, including a box of Romeo y Julieta Torpedos belonging to Sir Winston himself.

On St. James Street there are also toys that you can't slip into your suitcase—from the likes of William Evans, gun- and riflemaker (at St. James Street and St. James Place); the fine wine purveyors Justerini and Brooks; Berry Brothers and Rudd, another fine wine merchant; and Edmiston yacht sales.

## 24 Hackett

*Men's Clothing*

In the mere fifteen years since it was established, menswear retailer Hackett has managed to capture a lot of media and customer attention with its updated classics in natural fibers. Sweaters in unusual color combinations; shirts and jackets with a nip here and a tuck there. It's all properly British, but with a contemporary Euro touch that will pass muster at the firm or the barbecue. There's also a personal tailoring service. The Heathrow and Stansted airport locations offer tax-free shopping.

ADDRESS
89 Jermyn Street
SWI (Green Park Tube)

PHONE
0207 930 2885

HOURS
Mon.–Fri. 9:30 a.m.–6:00 p.m.;
Sat. 10:00 a.m.–6:00 p.m.

WEBSITE
www.hackett.co.uk
$$–$$$

BRANCHES:

SLOANE SQUARE
137 Sloane Street
SWI (Sloane Square Tube)

PHONE
0207 730 3331

COVENT GARDEN
30–31 King Street
WC2 (Covent Garden Tube)

PHONE
0207 240 2040

REGENT STREET
147 Regent Street
WIB (Piccadilly Circus Tube)

PHONE
0207 494 1855

(WITHIN SELFRIDGE'S)
400 Oxford Street
WIA (Marble Arch Tube)

PHONE
0207 629 1234 (ext. 2714)

(WITHIN HARVEY NICHOLS)
109–125 Knightsbridge
SWIX (Knightsbridge Tube)

PHONE
0207 201 8499

THE CITY
117 Bishopsgate
EC2 (Liverpool Street Tube)

PHONE
0207 626 7020

THE CITY
26 Eastcheap
EC3M (Liverpool Street Tube)

PHONE
0207 626 0707

LONDON HEATHROW
AIRPORT
Terminal 4

PHONE
0208 745 2579

STANSTED AIRPORT
PHONE
0127 966 1411

ADDRESS
77 and 97 Jermyn Street
W1 (Green Park Tube)

PHONE
0207 839 3578
$$

BRANCH:
55 Knightsbridge
SW1

PHONE
0207 235 2651

## 25  Harvie & Hudson
*Shirtmaker, Men's Clothing*

Harvie & Hudson is one of the many highly accomplished shirtmakers in the area (*see the sidebar on page 36*). I include it because I found a fantastic value there on a very useful item: a £99 Meyer unlined cotton jacket, nicely made (the seams are taped) and perfect for packing—just shake it out, then put it on with jeans or khakis when you want a bit of smartening up.

# CULTURE ALONG THE WAY

## Handel House Museum

At 23 and 25 Brooke Street, which runs between South Molton Lane and New Bond Street, is Handel House Museum, a good stop for visitors who like their museum-going in small doses.

Composer George Frederick Handel lived here from the time he leased the newly built house in 1723 until his death in 1759. While here, he composed the *Messiah* and *Music for the Royal Fireworks,* among many other works. He was a parishioner at nearby St. George's Church on Hanover Square, where he had his own pew.

The house has been restored to the way it would have appeared during Handel's life, and among other items, you can see in his sleeping quarters a bed that was luxurious for the period, and get his view through the red curtains to busy and fashionable Brook Street.

Music fans should also note that rock guitarist Jimi Hendrix lived in the house in 1968. This portion of the house, which is technically No. 23, is used for ever-changing exhibitions related to Handel's life and music. Check the website before your visit to find out what is showing. Admission: £4.50 adults; £2 children

ADDRESS
23 and 25 Brooke Street
WIK (Bond Street Tube)

PHONE
0207 495 1685

HOURS
Closed Mon.
Tues.–Sat. 10:00 a.m.–6:00 p.m.
(open Thurs. until 8:00 p.m.)
Sun. 12:00 p.m.–6:00 p.m.

WEBSITE
www.handelhouse.org

## St. James Piccadilly

The Greek revival church of St. James Piccadilly is a wonderful stop on your way. Built by Christopher Wren and consecrated in 1684, the interior looks more like a grand university library (or a men's club, in keeping with the neighborhood) than a church.

The church has a full program of activities and events designed for the visitor. The Blake Society celebrates poet William Blake, who was baptized here, with monthly lectures, discussions, and visits to Blake sites. See the society's website (www.blakesociety.org.uk) for activities.

ADDRESS
197 Piccadilly
W1J (Piccadilly Circus or Green Park Tube)

WEBSITE
www.st-james-piccadilly.org

On Mondays, Wednesdays, and Fridays, the church hosts lunchtime recitals featuring young and established classical artists performing fifty-minute concerts.

The London Festival Orchestra is St. James's resident orchestra, performing occasional concerts. The church's website has a detailed listing of its daily activities and events.

The church courtyard is the site of an antique and collectibles market each Tuesday from 8:00 a.m. to 6:00 p.m., which is fun for browsing. From Wednesday to Saturday the courtyard has arts and crafts stalls (10:00 a.m.–6:00 p.m.), a good way to see some local craft offerings.

The church is set between Piccadilly and Jermyn Streets, about two hundred yards from Piccadilly Circus. Enter from either Piccadilly, through the courtyard, or Jermyn Street.

## Trocadero

ADDRESS
13 Coventry Street
W1D (Piccadilly Circus Tube)

PHONE
0906 888 1100
0207 434 0034 (cinema)

HOURS
10:00 a.m.–1:00 a.m. daily

Trocadero, at Piccadilly Circus, is a good stop for a rainy day, or for those traveling with older children. This entertainment complex includes two video arcades with simulator rides, dodgem cars, a bowling alley, a pool room, sports bar, shops of interest to young people, and a cinema. Be aware that it's customary in London to book advance tickets for films. There's a branch of the cute and clever gift shop Octopus here (*see page 103*), a Starbucks, a Rainforest Café, and much more.

# WHERE TO EAT

MAYFAIR/ST. JAMES IS home to many fine and exclusive dining spots that are destinations in themselves: Nobu, Langan's Brasserie, Gordon Ramsay at Claridge's, the Connaught (where Gordon Ramsay protégée Angela Hartnett is chef), the Dorchester Hotel Grill Room. If you want to be certain of a meal at one of these places, you should make reservations up to a month in advance, possibly before you leave the United States. Confirm your reservations when you arrive in the UK.

London dining prices are about 30 percent higher than the rest of England, which itself is more expensive than dining out in the U.S., so be prepared to pay for your experience: Langan's and the Dorchester Grill Room, at about £40 per person, are considered reasonable for a good meal in London. Dinner at Gordon Ramsay at Claridge's goes for about £60 per person, and an à la carte meal at the Connaught Hotel can cost up to £85 per head.

## Al Duca

Exceptionally good handmade Italian food in a contemporary, sleek dining room. Expect homemade pastas, such as reginetti with peas and bacon, tuna carpaccio, bresaolo, pan-fried shrimp, grilled vegetables, steaks, smoked pork, lamb, fish, and grilled chicken. Lunch is £17.50 for two courses; £20.50 for three. Dinner is £20 for two courses; £24 for three. They also offer pre- and post-theater menus (£13.50 for two courses; £16.50 for three), which is a good value. The wine list is as long as a novella. Reservations recommended.

ADDRESS
4 Duke of York Street
SW1

PHONE
0207 839 3090

HOURS
Lunch and dinner, Mon.–Sat.;
closed Sun.

## Café at Sotheby's

Café at Sotheby's is fun for entertainment and a meal all in one. Browse the galleries at Sotheby's that display items for upcoming auctions. You can be sure the cases will be full of fascinating objects. It's like a mini-museum.

Then step into the very good café for breakfast, lunch, or tea. True, a lobster sandwich is £16.95, and the lamb rump with white beans is £16.50. But for only £5, you could have the exceptionally good soup, and a

ADDRESS
34–35 New Bond Street
W1A

PHONE
0207 293 5077

HOURS
Breakfast is served 9:30 a.m.–11:00 a.m.; lunch 12:00 p.m.–3:00 p.m.; tea 3:00 p.m.–4:45 p.m.

stir-fry will set you back only £7, as will the special. If you're feeling indulgent, Sotheby's has own-label champagne for £6.75 a glass.

## Carluccio's

ADDRESS
(in Fenwick department store, Bond Street)
PHONE
0207 629 0699
HOURS
Lunch only. The Market Place location, near Oxford Circus, is open for dinner.

BRANCH:
CARLUCCIO'S OXFORD CIRCUS
8 Market Place
WIN (Oxford Circus Tube)
PHONE
0207 636 2228

Carluccio's draws a crowd for lunch with their reliably good antipasti, pastas, and grilled foods, plus a small wine list and Italian desserts. The prices are very reasonable, with grilled lamb over spinach just £8.50, gnocchi baked in cheese with tomato sauce for £5.25, and spaghetti with white clam sauce for £6.50. There's a children's menu, too.

## Mo

ADDRESS
23 Heddon Street
WI (Oxford Circus Tube)
PHONE
0207 434 4040
HOURS
11:00 a.m.–11:00 p.m. daily
Food is served from noon to 10:00 p.m. on weeknights and until 10:30 p.m. from Thursday to Saturday.

Next door to the expensive and famous Moroccan restaurant Momo is the brilliant teahouse and bazaar Mo. Order hot or iced mint tea in gold cups to be served at low tables under hanging lanterns, or on cushiony stools outdoors in nice weather. The place is fun and atmospheric, decorated with Moroccan doodads and artifacts for sale, and serves very good mezze-type snacks from which you can make a meal. Individual tidbits such as hummus, baby potatoes, anchovy salad, and grilled eggplant cost £7 for a selection of four items. A bountiful family-size platter of homemade salads, spreads, dips, and meats is £30. Or just relax with something from the huge assortment of teas, coffees, and milk drinks.

## Momo

Momo, next door, is considered by many people to be one of London's great restaurant experiences. The décor is enchanting—entering the Momo is like stepping into Aladdin's cave. Diners generally find the food superb, but my London friends occasionally grumble about service and portion size at these prices. The downstairs bar, Kemia, is hopping, but you'll need to dress smartly to get in.

ADDRESS
25 Heddon Street
W1 (Oxford Circus Tube)

PHONE
0207 434 4040
Reservations required.

## Victory Café

On the lower ground floor (that's basement to you and me) of Gray's Mews Antiques is this little café, which serves fresh, cheap, homemade food. Nothing fancy here, but you can eat sausage or smoked haddock and mashed potatoes for £4.95; quiche for £2.95; ham, eggs, and fries for £3.95; or your choice of sandwiches. For entertainment, there's a free jukebox, and since the café is tucked among the antiques stalls, you can window-shop while you dine.

ADDRESS
1–7 Davies Mews
W1K (Bond Street Tube)

PHONE
0207 499 6801

HOURS
Mon.–Fri. 10:00 a.m.–5:30 p.m.

## Quaglino's

Quaglino's was bought some years back by Sir Terence Conran, zillionaire founder of Conran's and Habitat. After successful careers in the furniture business, garden business, and book business (he's authored or coauthored about fifty books), Sir Terence is in the food business—he has many London restaurants, all of them good to great (*see Bluebird, page 144; Orrery, page 184; and Café Mezzo/Mezzonine, page 170*).

Quaglino's is very big and busy. The crowds come for fresh, seasonal modern European/Mediterranean food that's usually quite good without being too gourmet. If you live in a large U.S. city, you've undoubtedly eaten plenty of food like that served at Quaglino's, but

ADDRESS
16 Bury Street
SW1 (Green Park Tube)

PHONE
0207 930 6767

it's not so usual in England, which is what has made it such a success.

Choices include English offerings such as roast fowl, lamb shanks, and vegetable lasagna, but the menu is dominated by fish and seafood, and these are usually the best choices. Since the place is big (and sometimes hectic and noisy) by English standards, it's a good choice for a group. Expect to pay about £30 per person without wine.

## Shepherd's Market

Make an evening of an excursion to Shepherd's Market, a charming little courtyard tucked away off Curzon Street. The narrow alleys and central court include several good restaurants and a pub, **Ye Grapes**, a fun, pretty place full of locals and decorated with crimson drapes and velvet stools. For midpriced French food in a cozy spot that's bustling and sometimes crowded, try **Le Boudin Bleu** (phone: 0207 499 3292). Or go the budget route with dinner at the **Market Brasserie**, next to Ye Grapes, where two courses cost only £8.50. **The Village** is a tiny, adorable spot offering such fare as sausages and pastas at reasonable prices.

The Lebanese restaurant **Al Hamra**, around the corner, has been a favorite stop since 1984. It offers friendly service and very good, authentic Lebanese food and wine. It's big enough that you possibly can get in without a reservation (still, it's always a good idea to make one). Expect a starter, main course, wine, and coffee to cost around £35 per person.

Before or after dinner, take a stroll around the shops in the courtyard and along Curzon Street.

To get to Shepherd's Market, walk down Piccadilly along Green Park. Take either Half Moon Street or Clarges Street to Curzon. Turn left on Curzon and walk a block or two until you find the entrance to Shepherd's Market.

# KNIGHTSBRIDGE AND SLOANE SQUARE

$\mathcal{E}$LEGANT KNIGHTSBRIDGE HAS ALL the elements for a well-rounded London experience: great hotels, proximity to museums, pretty churches, and enjoyable strolling. Due south from the Knightsbridge Tube station, Sloane Square is a remnant of the exclusive, understated, upper-crust England you find more often in old movies than in today's Cool Britannia. Between and around these points, you can give your wallet a workout in an area dense with designer shops, boutiques, and couturiers—not to mention Harrods and Harvey Nichols.

## WHERE TO STAY

### Knightsbridge Green

This family-owned hotel is a real find in pricey Knightsbridge. The twenty-eight rooms are a generous size by London standards, and thirteen of them have a separate lounge. Baths are newly refurbished and respectably large. Satellite TV, air conditioning, fax service, breakfast service, and access to a nearby health club are among the amenities. Hyde Park is nearby, and the hotel is a block from Harrods. Rates: singles from £110; doubles from £145; suites from £170.

ADDRESS
159 Knightsbridge
SW1

PHONE
0207 584 6274

E-MAIL
theKGHotel@aol.com

ADDRESS
189 Queensgate

## Gore Hotel

Situated between Knightsbridge and Kensington in Museumland, this is convenient to all three, if you enjoy a bit of walking. See page 107 for full description.

ADDRESS
4 Queensgate

## John Howard Hotel

Moderately priced rooms also in Museumland. See page 108 for full description.

ADDRESS
75 Sloane Street
SW1

PHONE
0207 235 7141

WEBSITE
www.cadogan.com

## The Cadogan

The Cadogan sits on the corner of Pont and Sloane, halfway between Sloane Square and Knightsbridge Tube stations, so it's ideally positioned for shopping. It's quite pretty, with the kind of big, comfortable sitting room that English hotels do so well. The rooms are average size but nicely decorated in a traditional style.

Opened as a hotel in 1887, the hotel soon became associated with two very famous people: Lillie Langtry and Oscar Wilde. Langtry, a famous actress and confidante of King Edward VII, lived at 21 Pont from 1892 to 1897. Her house was eventually sold to the hotel, but she retained her room long after the sale. Her drawing room and dining room, decorated with Prince of Wales feather plasterwork, are part of the hotel's facilities.

If you ask, hotel staff will show you (or even rent you) room 118, where Oscar Wilde was arrested after losing a civil libel action suit against the Marquess of Queensbury. He was jailed for two years for offenses against young men.

The dining room doubles as a meeting and party space. Guests at the Cadogan can use the private gardens and tennis court opposite the hotel.

Rates: singles from £140; luxury singles from £215; doubles from £225; Oscar Wilde room £300; suites begin at £325. Breakfast is extra.

## Sloane Hotel

The Sloane Hotel is strategically situated for shopping the parts of Knightsbridge nearest Chelsea. Knightsbridge Road itself is a twenty-minute walk down primo shopping streets Kings Road and Sloane. Much nearer are Sloane Square, Draycott Avenue, and Walton Street (*see page 56*). See page 127 for full description.

**ADDRESS**
29 Draycott Place
SW3

**PHONE**
Toll-free in the U.S.: 800-324-9960; 0207 581 5757 in England

**WEBSITE**
www.sloanehotel.com

## Knightsbridge and Sloane Square Shopping Areas

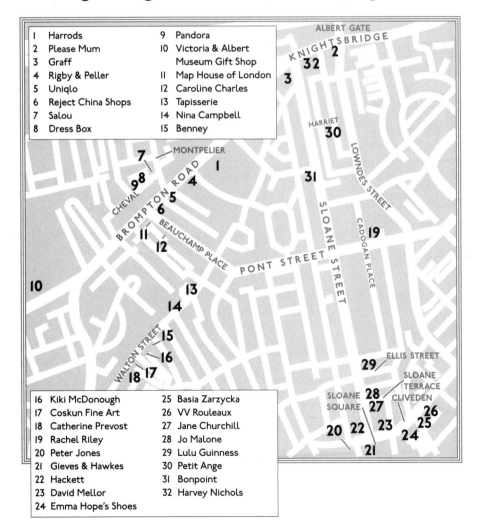

1 Harrods
2 Please Mum
3 Graff
4 Rigby & Peller
5 Uniqlo
6 Reject China Shops
7 Salou
8 Dress Box
9 Pandora
10 Victoria & Albert Museum Gift Shop
11 Map House of London
12 Caroline Charles
13 Tapisserie
14 Nina Campbell
15 Benney

16 Kiki McDonough
17 Coskun Fine Art
18 Catherine Prevost
19 Rachel Riley
20 Peter Jones
21 Gieves & Hawkes
22 Hackett
23 David Mellor
24 Emma Hope's Shoes
25 Basia Zarzycka
26 VV Rouleaux
27 Jane Churchill
28 Jo Malone
29 Lulu Guinness
30 Petit Ange
31 Bonpoint
32 Harvey Nichols

# KNIGHTSBRIDGE SHOPS

ADDRESS
87–135 Brompton Road
SW1 (Knightsbridge Tube)

PHONE
0207 730 1234

HOURS
Mon.–Sat. 10:00 a.m.–7:00 p.m.
(Should you forget that Harrods is
closed Sundays, you'll be reminded
by a helpful sandwich board in the
Knightsbridge Tube station.)

WEBSITE
www.harrods.com

## 1    Harrods

*Department Store*

Shopping in London for many people means shopping
at Harrods. The store should be seen for its sheer,
mind-boggling size and scope—more than three hundred departments and twenty restaurants cover a million
square feet. Doormen helpfully point you to the right
door for your destination, where other doormen will
whisk the doors open for you. Your first stop should be
picking up a store guide to navigate, or you'll walk
around lost all day.

The food hall is the main attraction for many shoppers. I can never resist the chocolate counters, offering
the wares of several different chocolatiers. But there are
329 other departments, too, including home décor,
bedding, and silver offerings, though these seem a little
ordinary for the price. Same goes for the cosmetics, stationery, fine jewelry, and accessories. (For instance, I
found a £52 headband identical to the $15 one I was
wearing.)

However, Harrods is rather good for souvenirs. Harrods World, on the fourth floor, has golf balls, hand
towels, T-shirts, and tins emblazoned with the gold
Harrods logo, which might be just what someone wants.
It's tax-free, too.

Harrods is also a good destination for those traveling
with children. The toy department is mammoth, as
good a toy store as you'll find in England, if volume is
what you're looking for. Several of the restaurants are
child-friendly. The deli is the best of them, and the ice
cream parlor on the fourth floor is also a great destination. And though Planet Harrods is everything you left
the U.S. to escape—chicken fingers and french fries
accompanied by kids' movies—you might be glad for it
after a long morning of shopping.

See the Harrods website to plan your visit.

## 2   Please Mum

*Children's Clothing and Evening Wear*

Please Mum stands out in a city of high-end children's shops for its designer styles and children's handmade ball gowns. Little Versace and Moschino outfits are still in plastic under signs reminding you not to touch. So leave the kids at home, because their little hands won't be able to keep away from the buttery leathers and satiny ball gowns. But bring the credit card with the highest limit.

ADDRESS
85 Knightsbridge
SW1 (Knightsbridge Tube)

PHONE
0207 486 1380

HOURS
Mon.–Sat. 10:00 a.m.–6:30 p.m.;
Sun. 10:00 a.m.–6:00 p.m.
$$

BRANCH:
24 Orchard Street
W1 (Marble Arch Tube)

PHONE
0207 486 3399

---

### ABOUT ENGLISH FLOOR LEVELS

If you walk into a store at street level in England, you are on the ground floor. The next floor up is the first floor. Below is the basement, usually referred to as the lower ground floor. The American elevator system uses 1 for the ground floor, the English system begins with 0 for the ground floor.

---

## 3   Graff

*Jewelry*

So enormous are the baubles at this internationally famous jeweler that I once tried on a small, affordable-looking ring that turned out to have 3.25 total karats of diamonds and cost £18,000, not including tax. The jewels are so big that the store brochure is oversized to show them full size: emerald and diamond earrings two inches long; nine-karat yellow diamonds as big as your thumbnail. The guard and doorman are not everyone's idea of a relaxed shopping experience, but where else are you going to experience jewelry like this?

ADDRESS
55 Brompton Road
SW3 (Knightsbridge Tube)

PHONE
0207 584 8571

HOURS
Mon.–Fri. 9:00 a.m.–5:30 p.m.;
Sat. 9:00 a.m.–5:00 p.m. ·

WEBSITE
www.graffdiamonds.com

BRANCHES:
11 Sloane Street
SW1X (Knightsbridge Tube)

PHONE
Same as Knightsbridge Store

6–7 New Bond
W1S (Oxford Circus Tube)

PHONE
Same as Knightsbridge Store

ADDRESS
2 Hans Road
SW3 (Knightsbridge Tube)

PHONE
0207 589 9293

HOURS
Mon.–Sat. 9:30 a.m.–6:00 p.m.
(open Wed. until 7:00 p.m.)

E-MAIL:
sales@rigbyandpeller.com
$$

BRANCHES:
22A Conduit Street
W1 (Oxford Circus Tube)

PHONE
0207 491 2200

HOURS
Mon.–Sat. 9:30 a.m.–6:00 p.m.
(open Thurs. until 7:00 p.m.)

HEATHROW AIRPORT
Terminal 3 Airside
TW6

PHONE
0208 757 3243

HOURS
6:00 a.m.–9:45 p.m. daily

## 4   Rigby & Peller
*Lingerie and Swimwear*

Corsetmaker to the queen and the late Queen Mother, Rigby & Peller is easy to find in its prime spot next to Harrods. This family-run business produces made-to-measure beautiful bras (£235 each) and corsets. They also carry an absolutely outstanding selection of other divine underthings. There are also specialty bras (gel bras, silicone enhancers) and lovely sleepwear, some of it made on-site. The staff is helpful and legendarily well-trained.

Rigby & Peller sells swimwear year-round, with tops and bottoms sold separately, so you can mix and match sizes for a perfect fit. The fabric choices for the swimwear are strangely unappealing, though, for the premium prices.

This location keeps much of its stock in drawers, which you slide open and rummage through, pretty much like home. The browsing is better at the Conduit Street location, where all the merchandise is out on racks. The July sale is well attended, as prices for this premium lingerie are slashed.

## 5 Uniqlo
*Men's, Women's, and Children's Clothing*

Basic, stylish, and very inexpensive clothing, this is Japan's version of the Gap, but less world-dominating. Good if your luggage is lost or delayed—you can pick up jeans, twill trousers (£20), T-shirts (from £7), tops, and casual collared shirts for men (£15), women, and children. Be sure to check the sale rack. I found a pair of children's jeans for an unheard-of £7. Uniqlo is also good for inexpensive jackets, should the English weather catch you unprepared. See a small selection of their wares on the website.

ADDRESS
163–169 BROMPTON ROAD
SW3 (Knightsbridge Tube)

PHONE
0207 584 8608

HOURS
Mon.–Sat. 10:00 a.m.–7:00 p.m. (open Wed. and Thurs. until 8:00 p.m.); Sun. 12:00 p.m.–6:00 p.m.

WEBSITE
www.uniqlo.co.uk
$

## 6 Reject China Shops
*China*

Although there is more first-quality china here than seconds, Reject China Shops are still good for popping in to see whether they have any seconds of your pattern. The seconds are clearly signed, and are the better buy.

If you buy on sale or buy seconds, it's never more expensive than china shopping in the States, especially if you spend more than £100, the minimum here for a tax refund. (*See page 12.*) Another compelling reason for UK china shopping is that the selection of patterns, and of dish types within patterns, is often better.

You'll find a set of six Portmeirion mugs for £48; Wedgwood dessert plates for £8.10; teacups for £11.10. If you are intent on getting a bargain, visit during the January and July sales for the biggest discount.

There are two branches of Reject China Shops in London, and each carries different lines, so if you're looking for something specific, you may wish to call before you go.

ADDRESS
183 Brompton Road
SW3

PHONE
0207 581 0739

E-MAIL:
reject183@china.uk.com

BRANCH:
71 Regent Street
W1B (Piccadilly Circus Tube)

PHONE
0207 734 4915
$-$$

ADDRESS
6 Cheval Place
(Note: Cheval Place is just off
Brompton Road to the north.)
SW7 (Knightsbridge Tube)

PHONE
0207 581 2380

HOURS
Mon.–Sat. 10:00 a.m.–5:00 p.m.
$$–$$$

## 7  Salou

*Designer Clothing Consignment*

Knightsbridge is a part of town where some just won't wear a designer outfit twice. These glamorous castoffs are packed away each season to Salou and its Cheval Place neighbors (*see below*), "dress agencies" that sell lightly worn, high-fashion designer clothing. You might wish to sort through the rack of leather skirts, or maybe the masses of evening wear (strapless brown silk Calvin Klein evening dress, £199) will catch your eye. The high standards occasionally extend to the prices—perhaps you will find an Armani blazer for £130, but this year's Chanel suit could still cost £800, and a Hermes jacket is no bargain at £1,900. There are fine shoes, too: £60 will get you a pair of pink metallic Miu Miu mules.

ADDRESS
8 Cheval Place
SW7 (Knightsbridge Tube)

PHONE
0207 589 2240

HOURS
Mon.–Fri. 10:00 a.m.–6:00 p.m.;
Sat. 10:30 a.m.–6:00 p.m.
$$–$$$

## 8  Dress Box

*Designer Clothing Consignment*

The Dress Box is smaller than Salou but so choice. You are in serious consigner territory here: A visitor overheard a well-heeled woman arranging to ship clothing for consignment—from Riyadh, Saudi Arabia. Snap up one of the designer leather jackets from a rack of select specimens, or flex your wallet for a Christian Dior jacket (£350) and a Dior slip dress (£350).

## FASHION VOCABULARY

If you're looking for windproof trousers for a cycling trip, for goodness' sake, don't prance into a British store and ask for plastic pants. "Pants" are underwear in England, and "plastic pants" is the term for an item worn over a cloth diaper.

Most London retail employees understand American English, but you could run into difficulties. Here are some other American-to-English fashion translations:

purse = handbag
ladies' wallet = purse
ladies' underwear = knickers
jockey shorts = Y-fronts
underwear = pants
undershirt = vest
vest = jerkin or waistcoat
suspenders = braces
garters = suspenders
pants = trousers
hooded raincoat = anorak or mac
hose = tights

sweater = jumper (or "cardy"—a cardigan)
off-the-rack or ready-to-wear = off-the-peg
corset or merry widow = basque
sneakers = plimsolls
running shoes = trainers
And if you have a hair appointment:
pigtails = bunches
braids = plaits
bangs = fringe

## 9 Pandora

*Designer Clothing Consignment*

Pandora is the biggest by far of the consignment shops on this block and features a huge collection of coats, jackets, designer suits, dresses, shoes, and handbags from "Armani to Zilkha" (their literature advises), all less than two years old. The selection of evening wear is exceptional: a twelve-foot rack of short evening dresses and a fifteen-foot rack of long evening dresses. Plentiful handbags, too, that hang from ceiling fixtures (Prada and Gucci handbags, around £117 to £160). Other finds included a supple Gucci leather jacket for £470, an Escada knit trouser suit for £117, and several Alberta Ferretti coats from £282.

ADDRESS
16 Cheval Place
SW7 (Knightsbridge Tube)

PHONE
0207 589 5289

HOURS
Mon.–Sat. 10:00 a.m.–5:00 p.m.
$$

ADDRESS
Cromwell Road
SW7 (South Kensington Tube)

PHONE
0207 942 2687

HOURS
Mon.–Sun. 10:00 a.m.–5:45 p.m.
(open Wed. and the last Fri. of the
month until 10:00 p.m.)

WEBSITE
www.vandashop.co.uk

$

## 10 Victoria & Albert Museum Gift Shop

*Souvenirs, Gifts, Crafts, Artisanal Jewelry*

Give yourself some time to browse the V&A gift shop's extensive offerings for tasteful souvenirs and all-round great gifts. Fill your suitcase with handsome, well-designed everyday objects like sleek scissors (£6.95) and long, slim, compact playing cards (£6.95) for giving. For something more English, try the beautiful reproduction tin plates, a fantastic bargain at £3.95 and guaranteed not to break in your suitcase, or wrapping paper and napkins printed with images from the museum collection. There are also Ossie Clark–designed shirts, replicas of Tudor handbags, and jewelry. The online catalog lists just a fraction of what is in the shop.

At the back of the Victoria & Albert Museum gift shop is a special space set aside for the Crafts Council Shop, which will knock your socks off. England's best craft artists are represented here, in cases and cases of indescribably original and highly desirable jewelry, handmade handbags, velvet scarves, teapots, and works in glass. It's absolutely worth budgeting some time and money to find yourself a one-of-a-kind item by one of England's many fine handcrafters. (Phone: 0207 942 8077; hours: Mon.–Sun. 10:00 a.m.–5.45 p.m.; open Wed. and the last Friday of the month until 10:00 p.m.; $–$$)

# BEAUCHAMP PLACE
## (JUST OFF BROMPTON ROAD TO THE SOUTH)

THIS LITTLE street is dense with couture shops—**Bruce Oldfield, Isabell Kristensen**—and other fine retailers, such as the **Janet Reger** lingerie shop, women's clothing designer **Paul Costelloe**, and **Dower & Hall** jeweler. **Venetia Studium** sells Fortuny pleated tops, gowns, and scarves and Fortuny lamp shades. **Bertie Golightly** is a top-drawer designer clothing reseller. Toward the intersection of Beauchamp and Walton is the fashionable **San Lorenzo** restaurant.

## 11  Map House of London
*Historic and Antique Maps*

Map House is a good place to lose yourself in the hundreds of maps of England and its counties, Scotland, Europe, the Americas, and farther flung corners of the globe. A casual browse could last for hours. If you know what you want, ask the staff to show you how the drawers are arranged. Pick up something for as little as £30, something more in the collector range, or something in between. The website has a comprehensive listing of its holdings, with photographs of recent acquisitions.

ADDRESS
54 Beauchamp Place
SW3 (Knightsbridge Tube)

PHONE
0207 589 4325

HOURS
Mon.–Fri. 9:45 a.m.–5:45 p.m.;
Sat. 10:30 a.m.–5:00 p.m.

WEBSITE
www.themaphouse.com
$–$$$

## 12  Caroline Charles
*Women's Fashion*

For more than thirty years, this shop has been a reliable source of luxurious clothing for London's well-dressed women. Caroline Charles revives classic town and country looks with luxurious, gorgeous fabrics, beautiful cuts, and flattering styling. If you believe a good jacket makes an outfit, you will adore Caroline Charles clothing. Prices are high, but you're paying for the fabric and workmanship rather than the label. You'll find items such as a quilted and patched silk jacket with detailed hand-sewing, £1,295; reversible black wool quilt-stitched brocade and leopard-print coat, £800; appliquéd box-shape cardigan with frog closures, £275. Some of the clothing is available at Harvey Nichols, Selfridge's, and Harrods.

ADDRESS
56 Beauchamp Place
SW3 (Knightsbridge Tube)

PHONE
0207 225 3197

HOURS
Mon.–Sat. 10:00 a.m.–6:00 p.m.;
open Wed. until 6:30 p.m.
$$$

# WALTON STREET

THE END of Beauchamp intersects Walton Street. One end of Walton runs into the back of Harrods, while the section between Beauchamp and Draycott has lots of specialty shops and boutiques. Toward the end of Walton, it's probably more convenient to use the South Kensington Tube.

ADDRESS
54 Walton Street
SW3 (Knightsbridge Tube)

PHONE
0207 581 2715

HOURS
Mon.–Fri. 10:00 a.m.–5:30 p.m.;
Sat. 10:00 a.m.–4:00 p.m.

WEBSITE
www.tapisserie.co.uk
$$

## 13  Tapisserie
*Needlework*

Step into this pretty shop (and get a look at the tiny garden out back) for high-end hand-painted needlework canvases and thread. Of note here are the Lulu Guinness and Anya Hindmarch handbag kits with an adorable retro look. You stitch the canvas, then Tapisserie makes it into a purse. Guinness canvases are priced from £100 to £200, and the making-up service is an additional charge of around £160 to £260. Have a look at the selection of canvases on the website.

ADDRESS
9 Walton Street
SW3 (Knightsbridge Tube)

PHONE
0207 225 1011

HOURS
Mon.–Sat. 10:00 a.m.–6:00 p.m.

WEBSITE
www.ninacampbell.com
$–$$$

## 14  Nina Campbell
*Furniture, Home Décor, Fabric*

The prolific designer's updated English brocade, linen, and silk fabrics are the current look in London's fashionable hotel rooms, including the Connaught Hotel and the Admiral Codrington pub in Chelsea.

The Walton Street shop is more oriented toward gifts and décor than fabric and trim. A few select pieces of furniture are augmented with other décor and tabletop items: pretty glassware and dishes, gorgeous cutlery, fabric bags, lamb's-wool throws, mirrors. You'll get loads of inspiration from her ideas. I loved the old crocodile suitcase topped with glass and made into a table. The shop also has fabric, wallpaper, and trim books, but no samples are available. Campbell's fabrics and other products are sold in the States, but generally only through the design trade. Get a preview on the website.

## Bridge Studios

Bridge Studios, Nina Campbell's London showroom, is open to the public. Pore over the examples of rooms decorated with Campbell fabrics, trim, wallpaper, paint, carpet, and table linens, and then order. Delivery takes a day or two, and you'll have to figure out the shipping. The location is well off the tourist trail, so you'll need a taxi or bus.

ADDRESS
318 Wandsworth Bridge Road
SW6

PHONE
0207 471 4270

HOURS
Mon.–Fri. 9:00 a.m.–6:00 p.m.;
Sat. 10:00 a.m.–4:00 p.m.

## 15 Benney
*Jewelry*

This jewelry and bauble maker holds four royal warrants for gold and silversmithing, and everything you'll see is designed and made by the shop. Amid the contemporary silver candlesticks and teapots and limited edition watches is a real bargain. Benney produces a line of bangles, chokers, and earrings of 23-karat gold over silver that make a bold statement at a modest price—about £380 for a bangle, or one-third the cost of an all-gold bangle. The bonding is said to last for years.

ADDRESS
73 Walton Street
SW3 (South Kensington Tube)

PHONE
0207 589 7002

HOURS
Mon.–Sat. 10:00 a.m.–5:00 p.m.
$$–$$$

## 16 Kiki McDonough
*Jewelry*

McDonough uses brightly colored semiprecious stones to make playful, colorful jewelry that's distinctive, eye-catching, and more reasonably priced than you might expect. I found a yellow gold bangle studded with amethyst, blue topaz, and peridot polka dots for £2,100. A bracelet of peridot, smoked quartz, and turquoise that looks like glass beads and is casual enough for everyday wear goes for £375. Get a look at her whimsical approach to jewelry-making on the website.

ADDRESS
77C Walton Street
SW3 (South Kensington Tube)

PHONE
0207 581 1777

HOURS
Mon.–Fri. 10:00 a.m.–6:00 p.m.;
Sat. 10:00 a.m.–5:00 p.m.

WEBSITE
www.kikimcd.com
$$–$$$

ADDRESS
93 Walton Street
SW3 (South Kensington Tube)

PHONE
0207 581 9056

HOURS
Mon.–Sat. 10:00 a.m.–6:00 p.m.

WEBSITE
www.coskunfineart.com

$$$

## 17 Coskun Fine Art
*Art Gallery*

Another of London's many fantastic art galleries, Coskun carries prints, drawings, and sculpture by American, British, and European masters of the twentieth century. The walls are covered with works from the greats: Picasso and Matisse drawings; early drawings by Andy Warhol, as well as his signature prints; Roy Lichtenstein's cartoony panels; and more from Francis Bacon and Lucien Freud. If you're not in the market for art, they're still nice about letting you look around. For a sample of what is on the walls, see the website.

ADDRESS
109 Walton Street
SW3 (South Kensington Tube)

PHONE
0207 584 8860

HOURS
Mon.–Fri. 10:00 a.m.–6:00 p.m.;
Sat. 10:00 a.m.–5:30 p.m.

$–$$$

## 18 Catherine Prevost
*Jewelry*

Jewelry design here is inspired by the qualities of the stones themselves. Prevost necklaces, in particular, are formed of strings of large, lightly shaped, and polished stones. The look is natural and dramatic, just the thing to accent a plain flowing linen dress or a swirly skirt. Other pieces are more refined, such as a wrap-style necklace of small tourmaline and faceted ruby drops (£475), suited to day or evening.

Those on a modest budget should look for the basket of bracelets in the corner. These are elastic-strung, polished semiprecious beads—tiger-eye, ebony, amethyst, smoked quartz, and more—and are a bargain at around £50.

# BROMPTON CROSS

WALTON STREET runs into Brompton to form a busy corner known as Brompton Cross, which has a choice selection of designer boutiques: **Jimmy Choo, Jean Paul Gaultier, Betsy Johnson, Paul & Joe**, as well as the romantic **Daphne's** Italian restaurant (a favorite of Diana Princess of Wales and a celeb-spotting venue) and **Bibendum**, an immense and pricey Conran restaurant.

# PONT STREET

WHEN BEAUCHAMP crosses Walton Street, it changes to Pont Street. Pont runs down to Belgravia Square, and near here are some pretty shops, including **Favourbrook** fine clothing for men and women; **Anya Hindmarch**'s luscious (and expensive) shoes and handbags; **Liza Bruce**, for handmade clothing; **Allegra Hicks**, for fabric, home, and clothing designs; **Agent Provocateur** for sexy lingerie.

## 19  Rachel Riley
### *Women's and Children's Clothing*

Smaller than the store on Marylebone, this location has a reasonable selection of styles, including items made from Liberty fabrics and great-looking suits. Be sure to look atop the shelves for marked-down items. See page 180 for a full description.

ADDRESS
13 Pont Street
SWI (Sloane Square Tube)

PHONE
0207 259 5969

HOURS
Mon.–Sat. 10:00 a.m.–6:00 p.m.
$–$$

# WHERE TO EAT

ADDRESS
151 Knightsbridge
SW1 (Knightsbridge Tube)

PHONE
0207 589 7347

HOURS
Lunch, 12:30–2:45 p.m.
Dinner, 7:00–11:45 p.m.

## Mr. Chow

Not as groundbreaking and hip as it seemed in the 1970s before every English village had a Chinese restaurant, but still, it's very good food in a stylish atmosphere without a heaving crowd. This is Chow's original restaurant (there are several now, mostly in America), and it was a big success, bringing in the likes of Marlene Dietrich, Mick Jagger, and the Beatles for Beijing classics such as green prawns, Peking duck, chicken satay, and noodle dishes.

Early in his career, Michael Chow began to commission portraits of himself from the artists dining in his restaurants: Keith Haring, Helmut Lang, Andy Warhol, and Julian Schnabel. He became well-known for his art collection, pieces of which hang on the walls of the Knightsbridge restaurant. The art aside, it's a skillfully designed space. Chow later designed an Armani boutique in Beverly Hills, and then another in the Bellagio Hotel in Las Vegas.

Dumplings are around £5.50; Peking duck for two is £26 per person; red-cooked pork knuckle will set you back only £14; pork loin sel et poivre is £10.50; and a set two-course meal is £15; 3 courses for £18.

# Isola

If your taste runs to a bustling, trendy spot, head to Isola, next door to Mr. Chow.

Fresh, high-quality ingredients and authentically Italian treatment turn out food that diners love (while occasionally flinching at the cost). Prices are at the north end of the scale for Italian food in London. Starters like homemade beet ravioli or grilled artichoke with warm cheese and rocket are around £11. Entrées like steamed sea bass, lamb, and Italian pork belly go for £35.

The wine list is enormous—around three hundred bottles, of which several dozen are served by the glass.

The wall of Isola is glass, and you can look down into the restaurant from the sidewalk. You'll likely see that every table is full, so reservations are recommended.

ADDRESS
145 Knightsbridge
SW1 (Knightsbridge Tube)
PHONE
0207 838 1055

# Enterprise Bar & Restaurant

The Enterprise was once a pub and still looks it from the outside. Inside, though, it's an excellent restaurant run by the same team that runs the American grill Christopher's in Covent Garden (*see page 92*). There are always loads of Americans here, plus expensively dressed British ladies and businessmen ordering the likes of carpaccio, chicken breast and risotto, sausage and mashed potatoes, Caesar salad, and delicacies such as asparagus and lemon sorrel salad with quail eggs and mousseline of goat cheese. Expect a minimum of £20 with wine. Reservations are not accepted.

ADDRESS
35 Walton Street
SW3 (South Kensington Tube)
PHONE
0207 584 3148
HOURS
Lunch, 12:30–2:30 p.m.
Dinner, 6:00–10:00 p.m.

# Mima's Deli

Charming little Knightsbridge Green meanders between Knightsbridge Road and Brompton Road, inviting a wander. When you spot the line of customers, you'll know you're at Mima's. Fresh, best-quality ingredients are piled high on chewy bread, then toasted, if you wish, for an exceptionally good sandwich at around £3.50.

ADDRESS
9 Knightsbridge Green
SW1
PHONE
0207 589 6820
HOURS
Mon.–Sat. 6:00 a.m.–5:00 p.m.

They also have take-out salads and other goodies. If you prefer a hot meal, there's a short eat-in menu of pastas and English favorites, all under £5, that locals say is quite good.

## Other Dining Options

Harvey Nichols has a branch of **Wagamama**, the noodle shop (*see page 124*), on its lower ground floor. Use the Seville Street entrance.

Harrods has about twenty eateries, including a pub, an oyster bar, several cafés, a tapas bar, and a diner. Londoners say the deli is best, but families with small children likely will be drawn to **Mo's Diner** or **Planet Harrods**, where the little ones eat burgers or chicken fingers while adults can have a freshly made crêpe and a glass of wine. It's no gourmet meal, but you could do a lot worse, and the prices are reasonable.

# SHOPS ON SLOANE SQUARE AND SLOANE STREET TO HARVEY NICHOLS

ADDRESS
Sloane Square
SW1

PHONE
0207 730 3434

HOURS
Mon.–Sat. 9:30 a.m.–7:00 p.m.

## 20 Peter Jones
*Department Store*

Most people enter Sloane Square by walking down Sloane Street, or via the Tube stop in the square, which is opposite Peter Jones department store.

Somehow Sloane Square became ultra-chic, with its own habitué: a slim, wealthy, dyed-blonde woman or her equally well-heeled husband, known as a Sloane Ranger. Yet Peter Jones stayed modest. With a motto of "Never Knowingly Undersold," it's definitely not Selfridge's, and as such, not much of a tourist draw.

But there are three good reasons to shop here. For starters, the café on the top floor is very good, and very reasonably priced (*see page 72*). Peter Jones is well-known for its big selection of furnishing fabrics (including Nina Campbell, Osborne & Little, Jane Churchill, and

Liberty), many of which are made up into curtains or padded panels, which is useful in assessing your choices.

And for celebrity spotters, Peter Jones is a good bet for espying famous Londoners as they purchase lint brushes or cereal bowls.

## 21 Gieves & Hawkes

*Men's Clothing and Tailoring*

This respected men's clothing retailer and tailor business was formed when two firms, established in the eighteenth century, merged. It is actually based at 1 Savile Row and holds three royal warrants: one for the queen's livery, one for the Duke of Edinburgh, and one for the Prince of Wales.

This outlet offers best-quality ready-to-wear shirts, jackets, suits, coats, knitwear, and accessories, all put together by the well-trained staff.

ADDRESS
33 Sloane Square
SW1

PHONE
0207 730 1777

HOURS
Mon.–Sat. 9:30–6:00 p.m. (open Wed. until 7:00 p.m.); Sun. 11:00 a.m.–5:00 p.m.

BRANCHES:
No. 1 Savile Row
W1S

PHONE
0207 434 2001

THE CITY
House of Fraser
68 King William Street
EC4

PHONE
0870 160 7274

ADDRESS
137 Sloane Street
SW1

PHONE
0207 730 3331

## 22 Hackett
*Men's Clothing*

*(See page 37 for complete description.)*

ADDRESS
4 Sloane Square
SW1 (Sloane Square Tube)

PHONE
0207 730 4259

HOURS
Mon.–Sat. 9:30 a.m.–5:00 p.m.

WEBSITE
www.davidmellordesign.com
$$

## 23 David Mellor
*Kitchenware, Flatware*

David Mellor is primarily a kitchen store with quality, well-designed kitchen tools. But what draws me here is the stylish, functional flatware. The ten current designs are elegantly minimal but practical, and designed with ergonomics in mind. A six-piece place setting is typically around £100 for stainless steel, a little more for silver plate. To get a good look at the designs before you go to the store, visit the website.

ADDRESS
53 Sloane Square
SW1 (Sloane Square Tube)

PHONE
0207 259 9566

WEBSITE
www.emmahope.co.uk
$$$

BRANCH:
208 Westbourne Grove
W11 (Ladbroke Grove Tube)

PHONE
0207 212 7493

## 24 Emma Hope's Shoes
*Women's Shoes*

Emma Hope shoes are the darlings of the press and are the heels under London's well-heeled because although they're ravishing, they're also wonderfully wearable. Her fame began with brocade mules, and her collections still include examples such as a velvet mule embroidered with metal tape (£309), definitely something you should consider purchasing if you have been nominated for an Academy Award. Every season's collection doubtless includes something to make your heart beat fast, from beautiful suede pumps (£239) and suede loafers (£209), to striped velvet pumps (£239) and perforated leather boots (£349). Preview the current collection and previous seasons on the website.

If you can catch the July sale, you'll be rewarded with sharp discounts. The Westbourne Grove location had racks and racks of shoes on sale, many under £100 a pair.

## 25 Basia Zarzycka

*Fantasy Gowns, Evening Wear,*
*Wedding Gowns, Accessories*

ADDRESS
52 Sloane Square
SW1 (Sloane Square Tube)

PHONE
0207 730 1660

WEBSITE
www.basias.com
$–$$$$

Step into this shop and you feel like Gretel opening the chest in the witch's house, or some equally bedazzled creature in an eccentric fantasy. Every corner is jam-packed with ornamentation; every surface and every surface on those surfaces is decorated, beaded, appliquéd, tasseled, trimmed, dripping with ornaments, shimmering with jewels, or all of these things at once.

Basia Zarzycka, a Brit of Polish heritage, graduated from Goldsmith's College and opened her business in 1995 as a fashion, bridal, and accessories shop. Zarzycka's fantasy gowns, made to measure, start at £6,000. Naturally, you'll want matching shoes.

For the mother of the bride or other once-in-a-lifetime occasions, Zarzycka has matching shawls and bags worked with extraordinary detail. One bag and matching shawl featured floral garden lace with silk

flowers and tassels, and another featured appliquéd pansies (£895 for the pansy bag; £1,800 for the shawl).

For the casual shopper, the earrings and gorgeous hair ornaments, usually priced less than £30, are a good way to bring home a bit of the fantasy. See a sample of the gowns, shoes, and tiaras on the website.

ADDRESS
54 Sloane Square
SW1 (Sloane Square Tube)

PHONE
0207 730 3125

HOURS
Mon.–Sat. 9:30 a.m.–6:00 p.m.
(except Wed. 10:30 a.m.–6:30 p.m.)

WEBSITE
www.vvrouleaux.com

BRANCH:
6 Marylebone High Street
W1 (Regents Park Tube)

PHONE
0207 224 5179

HOURS
Mon.–Sat. 9:30 a.m.–6:00 p.m.
For the professional, VV Rouleaux
has a trade operation off
Wandsworth Bridge Road, south of
the river. By appointment only.
(Phone: 0207 627 4455)

## 26  VV Rouleaux
*Ribbons, Trims, Haberdasher*

Opened by former florist Annabel Lewis in the early 1990s, this ribbon shop now sets the standard for haberdashers with its fresh looks and sheer volume. If you can imagine it, they have it. The bins and shelves bulge with braids, cords, rusched ribbon, velvet trim, crocheted bits, laces, fringes of every description, tassels, leather ribbon, fabric and leather flowers, rosettes, fur-print trim, and luxurious metal-thread braid. Be inspired by the selection to buy something beautiful on impulse, or bring your fabric swatch to find something to match. See part of the offerings on the website.

## 27  Jane Churchill

*Fabric, Wallpaper*

Founder Jane Churchill has an awesome pedigree—she married into the Churchill family, and as well, her aunt transformed a fabric shop into Colefax & Fowler. She started, then sold, her own business selling fabrics and wallpaper. Though she's no longer at the helm, the firm still employs talented designers. The patterns run to checks, plaids, and traditional tidy florals, mostly the casual English country look.

ADDRESS
151 Sloane Street
SW1 (Sloane Square Tube)

PHONE
0207 730 9847

HOURS
Mon.–Sat. 9:30 a.m.–6:00 p.m.
$$

## 28  Jo Malone

*Bath and Fragrance*

Malone started out by giving facials to clients in her apartment, mixing her own preparations for each individual. The famous story about Malone is that she gave her early clients a complimentary bottle of Nutmeg and Ginger bath oil. One client ordered 100 bottles to give as party gifts. Of those 100 recipients, 86 called to order another bottle.

Her evocatively named fragrances are designed to be mixed and worn in combination to suit your mood or destination. Besides the original Nutmeg and Ginger, there is the bracing Lime Basil and Mandarin, Verbenas of Provence, Vetyver, Lavender, French Lime Blossom, Gardenia, Red Roses, the deep, intensely masculine Wild Fig and Cassis, and Fleurs de la Foret. Most are strong and clean-smelling and many have a unisex appeal. The fragrances are £27 for 30 ml. The bath oil is around £20 to £52, depending on the container. Body lotion is £20 for 100 ml.

There's also a line of mix-and-match skin products: cleansers, moisturizers, and "specialists" that address specific conditions. Face products range from £17 for avocado cleansing milk to £65 for a big tub of orange and geranium night cream. Facial treatments and relaxing arm massages available.

ADDRESS
150 Sloane Street
SW1 (Sloane Square Tube)

PHONE
0207 730 2100

HOURS
Mon.–Sat. 10:00 a.m.–6.00 p.m.
(open Wed. and Thurs. until 7:00 p.m.)
$–$$

BRANCHES:
23 Brook Street
W1K (Bond Street Tube)

PHONE
0207 491 9104

HOURS
Mon.–Sat. 10:00 a.m.–6:30 p.m.
(open Thurs. until 7:00 p.m.)

24 Royal Exchange
EC3 (Bank Tube)

PHONE
0207 444 1999

HOURS
Mon.–Fri. 9:30 a.m.–6:00 p.m.

ADDRESS
3 Ellis Street
SW1 (Sloane Square Tube)

PHONE
0207 823 4823

HOURS
Mon.–Sat. 10:00 a.m.–6:00 p.m.
$–$$

# 29 Lulu Guinness
*Handbags*

Though Lulu Guinness bags are available in Neiman Marcus, and in New York and Los Angeles, if you're a fan of these whimsical designs, you should drop by this shop for the comprehensive selection. Guinness's bags have caught the fancy of fashion editors and the stylish and starry, with their clever evocation of the 1950s in style and color: totes appliquéd with girlie images (£78), a handbag shaped like a flowerpot (£65) or a basket of strawberries, and a shoulder bag in the form of a fifties evening dress. Wherever your eye lands in the store, there'll be something clever or engaging, from the artful displays to the floor, which is made from pages of old *Vogue* magazines under plexiglas. Guinness's handbags are also available at Harvey Nichols, Harrods, Liberty, and Selfridge's in the UK.

# DOWN SLOANE STREET

Sloane Street toward Brompton Road/Knightsbridge is the best-known stretch of Sloane Street, and it rivals Bond Street for sheer density of international designers: **Hermes, Versace, Gucci, Dior, Yves St. Laurent, Fendi, Escada, Kenzo, Hilfiger**, and much more. But note that virtually everything in this stretch of retail is closed on Sunday, save the **Hugo Boss** store.

## 30  Petit Ange
*Children's Clothing*

In this beautiful shop, the premium-priced clothes are displayed in converted wardrobes under chandeliers. Petit Ange is available in limited distribution in the States, but if you haven't seen them, you'll faint over the gorgeous little clothes from newborn to twelve years.

ADDRESS
6 Harriet Street (off Sloane Street)
SW1 (Knightsbridge Tube)

PHONE
0207 235 7337

HOURS
Mon.–Sat. 10:00 a.m.–6:00 p.m.
$–$$

ADDRESS
35B Sloane
(just off the corner of Sloane)
SW1 (Knightsbridge Tube)

PHONE
0207 235 1441

HOURS
Mon.–Sat. 10:00 a.m.–6:00 p.m.
$–$$

BRANCHES:
38 Old Bond Street
W1 (Green Park Tube)

PHONE
0207 495 1680

17 Victoria Grove
W8 (Kensington High Street or
Gloucester Road Tube)

PHONE
0207 584 5131

197 Westbourne Grove
W11 (Notting Hill Gate or
Ladbroke Grove Tube)

PHONE
0207 792 2515

## 31 Bonpoint

*Children's Clothing*

Fashionable mums and indulgent grandmums head to Bonpoint to outfit their precious little ones in well-designed, smart clothing that rises above trendy. With only a half-dozen U.S. locations, most U.S. shoppers have not seen Bonpoint clothing, and it's well worth a look. It's also less expensive in London than in the States. The several Bonpoint shops in London carry different items for different ages. The Notting Hill shop (on Westbourne Grove) is slightly funkier than the Bond Street shop. The Kensington shop (on Victoria Grove) stocks merchandise for babies only.

## 32  Harvey Nichols

*Department Store*

**ADDRESS**
109–125 Knightsbridge
SW1E (Knightsbridge Tube)

**PHONE**
0207 235 5000

**HOURS**
Mon.–Fri. 10:00 a.m.–8:00 p.m.;
Sat. 9:30 a.m.–8:00 p.m.; Sun.
12:00 p.m.–6:00 p.m.

Harvey Nicks, as Londoners call it, opened originally as a linen store in 1813, and now battles it out with Self-ridge's for the title of London's most exclusive department store. Its foremost weapon in the struggle is three big floors of designer fashion, including Diane von Furstenburg, Stella McCartney, Michael Kors, Anne Klein, Miu Miu, YSL, the revamped Balenciaga, and the thrilling Alexander McQueen, among many others.

The ground floor features a vast array of makeup and beauty counters and a juice bar. There is a large shoe department of wildly impractical styles. The hair and beauty salons offer all the latest treatments.

The in-store children's boutique, Buckle My Shoe, features gorgeous clothes alongside children's Moschino, Buckle My Shoe, and Dolce & Gabbana shoes, should nothing be too good for your sweetums.

If you can get a table, the Fifth Floor restaurant has fiber-optic walls that change color; it is a very trendy place to be seen these days. It is open for lunch until 3:30 p.m. and dinner until 11:30 p.m. (except Sundays). If you can't get a table, there's also a Yo! Sushi on the fifth floor. And while you wait, the fifth floor has a small grocery store, where a single package of microwave pop-corn is £2.25.

# WHERE TO EAT

## Top Floor

ADDRESS
Sloane Square (inside Peter Jones)
SW1

PHONE
0207 730 3434

HOURS
Mon.–Sat. 9:30 a.m.–7:00 p.m.

The eatery at Peter Jones is a big, bright cafeteria-style brasserie with exceptionally good food at low prices. The food choices are multicultural: avocado and seared tofu salad with gazpacho dressing (£3.95); sushi; wild mushroom soup with roast chestnuts (£3.95); hot steak sandwich; pastas (around £9); panini; and a few meals of the pork chop or chicken breast variety. There's also an espresso bar, and wine and beer are available. Every time I go, I wish it were open for dinner.

## Oriel

ADDRESS
50 Sloane Square
SW1

PHONE
0207 730 2804

HOURS
8:30 a.m.–11:00 p.m. daily

Oriel is situated right on Sloane Square, so it's easy to find. Upstairs is a proper restaurant serving pastas, fish, chicken and such, mostly reasonably priced. It's jam-packed at lunch and in the evening, when the locals use it as a bar (although dinner is served). Expect a bill of around £30 per person for a full meal with wine. You will likely need a reservation.

Downstairs is a café with a smaller selection, including grilled salmon, grilled vegetable and mozzarella panini, steak panini, roast tomato and pesto salad, that sort of thing. Nothing downstairs costs more than £10.50.

# CULTURE ALONG THE WAY

HERE'S ONE route for a shopping stroll through Knightsbridge that takes a two-mile walk past or very near many of the shops detailed in this chapter. It's an excellent way to see it all.

From the Knightsbridge Tube station, take the Harrods exit and walk down Brompton Road. (At this point, you could detour into **Rigby & Peller** on Hans or the posh resale shops off Montpelier.) Take a left on Beauchamp Place to stroll past the many couture boutiques, then a right on Walton Street. Walton runs into Draycott Avenue, which has some very stylish shops and terrific eateries.

For the abbreviated version of the walk, turn right on Draycott, then quickly left onto Brompton and return to **Harrods**, with maybe a quick stop in the magnificent **Brompton Oratory** (*see page 74*).

For the full tour, turn left on Draycott and walk ten minutes to Kings Road. Take a left onto Kings Road and you'll be a ten-minute walk from Sloane Square. At Sloane Square, you are a ten-minute walk from **Harvey Nichols**, a walk that will take you past fine international designer shopping.

## Royal Court Theatre

This is the premier venue for new British playwriting. It has two theaters, Upstairs (smallish, often showing controversial or difficult plays) and Downstairs (the main stage). To find out what's on, call or visit the website.

There's a restaurant in the theater, Royal Court Bar and Food (phone: 0207 565 5061). It's run by the Digby Trout organization, which has its niche operating exceptional good-value eateries on the premises of arts and entertainment venues, including the London Zoo, Kensington Palace Orangery (*see page 123*), British Museum, and others. The food is freshly prepared and always good, and prices are very fair. Lunch and dinner are served. Reservations are a good idea at dinner.

ADDRESS
Sloane Square

PHONE
0207 565 5000

WEBSITE
www.royalcourttheatre.com

## Bonhams

ADDRESS
Montpelier Street
SW7 (Knightsbridge Tube)
PHONE
0207 393 3900
HOURS
Mon.–Fri. 9:00 a.m.–5:00 p.m.
WEBSITE
www.bonhams.com

This auction house is a fun stop for a bit of culture. When you pop in here, you never know what will be on view. Could be antique firearms, could be rock-'n'-roll memorabilia, could be Asian watercolors. Bonhams holds auctions nearly every day at this location and at the New Bond Street office. Items go on view two to three days before the auction, and strolling the viewings is fun, free, and open to the public. Auctions are scheduled up to six months in advance, so you can plan your Bonhams visit before you leave the States. Their website includes a calendar of auctions. Click on "sales" then "calendar."

## Brompton Oratory

ADDRESS
Brompton Road and Thurloe Place
SW7
WEBSITE
www.brompton-oratory.org.uk

No other church interior in England can prepare you for the Italianate exuberance of Brompton Oratory, the Roman Catholic church otherwise known as the London Oratory, and properly as the Congregation of the Oratory of Saint Philip Neri. Decoration and scale compete for your attention in this imposing edifice. Curiously enough, the design was developed as the result of a public contest in the 1870s. Some of the fittings actually are Italian, including the twelve marble apostles. Interior photos on the website are not especially illuminating but give you an idea of the grandeur.

A regular Monday night program of organ recitals at the Oratory is open to the public. Check the church's website for a schedule.

# COVENT GARDEN

*C*OVENT GARDEN'S LIVELY PIAZZA, street performers, and dense shopping are just part of its draw. The area also has wonderful winding streets to wander, plenty of eateries, excellent people-watching, museums and galleries, and, of course, theater.

## WHERE TO STAY

### Covent Garden Hotel

Opened in 1997, this sumptuous fifty-eight-room hotel has individually decorated rooms with fabulous bathrooms and an excellent restaurant, Brasserie Max. There's a large, warm and inviting drawing room where you can settle in with a newspaper or a nightcap, play cards, or just lounge in the overstuffed chairs and stare at the log fire. A multitude of facilities includes a gym, beauty treatment room, screening room, and private meeting and dining rooms. The service is first-rate, the concierge is a genius, and the location is prime real estate in the theater district. Single rooms are available from £195; doubles from £235; junior suites from £325. See the rooms and services on the website.

ADDRESS
10 Monmouth Street
WC2

PHONE
0207 806 1000

WEBSITE
www.firmdale.com

ADDRESS
4 Broad Court, Bow Street
WC2B

PHONE
0207 836 8305

WEBSITE
www.the-fielding-hotel.co.uk

# Fielding Hotel

If you don't need a big drawing room, concierge, or roaring fire, try the Fielding. You're across Bow Street from the opera house, and next to the Bow Street Magistrates Court in an attractive pedestrian courtyard surrounding the nineteenth-century building that houses the hotel. Clean, modest-size rooms in matching pine furniture open off narrow halls. All twenty-four rooms have private baths, TVs, and phones. The beds are suitable quality, and, all in all, it's good, basic accommodation in an ideal location at a great price for Covent Garden: singles, £76; and doubles, £100. The biggest rooms (double with a sitting room) are £130. Children over thirteen only.

## Covent Garden Shopping Area

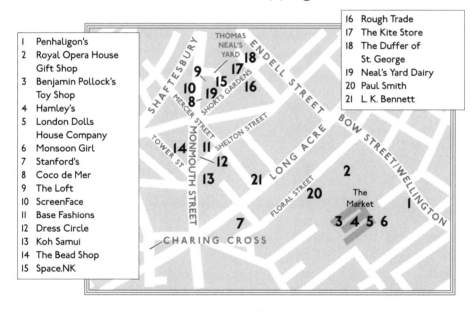

1. Penhaligon's
2. Royal Opera House Gift Shop
3. Benjamin Pollock's Toy Shop
4. Hamley's
5. London Dolls House Company
6. Monsoon Girl
7. Stanford's
8. Coco de Mer
9. The Loft
10. ScreenFace
11. Base Fashions
12. Dress Circle
13. Koh Samui
14. The Bead Shop
15. Space.NK
16. Rough Trade
17. The Kite Store
18. The Duffer of St. George
19. Neal's Yard Dairy
20. Paul Smith
21. L. K. Bennett

## THINGS TO KNOW ABOUT COVENT GARDEN

On Saturdays, the Covent Garden Tube stop permits exiting only between 1:00 p.m. and 5:00 p.m. To ride out of Covent Garden, you'll need to choose another stop. Leicester Square is the nearest at just a five-minute walk.

# SHOPPING

## 1 Penhaligon's
*Fragrance and Toiletries*

Begun by William Henry Penhaligon in the 1870s as an expansion of his barbershop, Penhaligon's became the royal barber, and the store still holds royal warrants from the Duke of Edinburgh and the Prince of Wales.

The Penhaligon's repertoire includes both classic and modern scents: old-style bracing fragrances, such as Blenheim Bouquet (Churchill's favorite); sweet old garden-gate fragrances such as Violetta and Bluebell; and newer, multinote fragrances such as Malabar. Most fragrances are available as eau de toilette, bath and shower gel, and body cream, and some additionally as bath oil, deodorant, shaving cream, dusting powder, and other treats. Eau de toilette sprays are priced starting at around £30 for 50 ml.

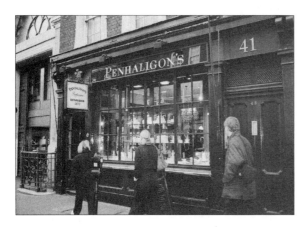

ADDRESS
41 Wellington Street
WC2 (Covent Garden Tube)

PHONE
0207 836 2150

HOURS
Mon.–Sat. 10:00–6:00 p.m. (open Thurs. and Sat. until 7:00 p.m.); Sun. 12:00 p.m.–6:00 p.m.
$

BRANCHES:
(besides these, there are branches in the City and Windsor)

MAYFAIR
20A Brook Street
W1K (Bond Street Tube)

PHONE
0207 493 0002

PICCADILLY
16 Burlington Arcade
W1J (Green Park or Piccadilly Circus Tube)

PHONE
0207 629 1416

(WITHIN HARRODS)
Brompton Place
SW1

PHONE
0207 730 1234

(WITHIN SELFRIDGE'S)
Oxford Street
W1C

PHONE
0207 318 2321

(WITHIN LIBERTY)
Regent Street
W1R

PHONE
0207 573 9506

ADDRESS
Bow Street
WC2 (Covent Garden Tube)

PHONE
0207 212 9331

HOURS
Mon.–Sat. 10:00 a.m.–7:30 p.m.

$

## 2   Royal Opera House Gift Shop
*Periodicals, Recordings, and Gifts*

A good stop for recordings, publications, and gifts for opera and ballet fans. Silverplate ROH barware, crystal decanters and flutes, opera glasses, Murano glass jewelry, dance and opera magazines, calendars. The shop carries plenty of specialist CDs. The video recordings of opera and ballet are tempting, but they are recorded in the European PAL format, which isn't compatible with U.S. videocassette players. Ask about the compatibility of the DVD format. (Note: Though the address of the opera house is Bow Street, the gift shop is actually just inside the Covent Garden market entrance.)

## The Market

The Covent Garden market stalls are fun to wander, especially if your schedule doesn't permit a trip to one of London's weekend markets.

The permanent market has some terrific shops worth stopping into:

ADDRESS
44 Covent Garden Market
WC2 (Covent Garden Tube)

PHONE
0207 379 7866

HOURS
Mon.–Sat. 10:00 a.m.–6:00 p.m.;
Sun. 11:00 a.m.–4:00 p.m.

WEBSITE
www.pollocks-coventgarden.co.uk.

$

## 3   Benjamin Pollock's Toy Shop
*Toys, Paper Theaters*

Since the nineteenth century, this small retailer has been the place to shop for paper theaters. Nowadays, these make inexpensive, iconic English gifts. Choose Shakespeare's Globe (£6.95), Punch & Judy (£3.95), Royal Opera House, or a kit that includes theater, characters, and text for a production of Cinderella (£6.95). Puppets, marionettes, finger puppets, and puppetry books are some of the other theatrical offerings.

Pollock's also has a large and engaging range of paper toys. Stock up on historic paper dolls of Queen Elizabeth I, Swinging '60s London, or Tudor times. Or choose an old-fashioned flip book. A table holds little bins of trinkets and toys inexpensive enough for children. We found a tiny hurdy-gurdy playing a bit of the Rolling Stones' "Satisfaction" (£3.99). Glass cases hold vintage toys.

## 4  Hamley's
*Toys*

A piddling outpost of the Regent Street emporium (*see page 99*), but sufficient if you're in need of a quick toy or a child-appeasing shopping stop.

ADDRESS
3 Covent Garden,
Central Market Hall
WC2

PHONE
0207 240 4646

WEBSITE
www.hamleys.com
$

## 5  London Dolls House Company
*Dollhouses and Accessories*

London Dolls House is enchanting fun for the browser and a temptation for the dollhouse enthusiast. Meticulous detail and styling characterize the houses here, from a grand Georgian to a half-timbered cottage. A large, intricately detailed dollhouse with authentic styling for £8,000 is the most expensive, but there are equally striking, less-expensive models, such as a thatched cottage for £2,245 and the art-deco International-style house for £1,995. Midpriced house kits cost around £300 (such as a Tudor half-timbered house for £250). There are also small house kits for less than £100.

If you're looking to redecorate, pore over the cases of furniture and accessories, including midcentury easy chairs, French fainting couches, wicker ensembles, and Chinese screens.

There are also building materials in dollhouse sizes and quantities, such as flooring, tiles, bricks slate, mantels, cornices, molding, ceiling roses, columns, and door surrounds. Their webpage, while not exhaustive, gives a good idea of what they offer, and includes an order form.

ADDRESS
29 Covent Garden Market
WC2 (Covent Garden Tube)

PHONE
0207 240 8681

HOURS
Mon.–Sat. 10:30 a.m.–7:00 p.m.;
Sun. 12:00 p.m.–5:00 p.m.

WEBSITE
www.london-dolls-house.sagenet
.co.uk/default.htm
(Note: £100 minimum for
VAT reclaim)
$–$$$$

ADDRESS
25 Covent Garden Market
WC2 (Covent Garden Tube)

PHONE
0207 497 9325

HOURS
Mon.–Sat. 10:00 a.m.–8:00 p.m.;
Sun. 11:00 a.m.–6:00 p.m.

WEBSITE
www.monsoon.co.uk
$

## 6  Monsoon Girl
*Girls Clothing and Accessories*

Monsoon for big girls specializes in floating, shimmering, jeweled clothing, an aesthetic that extends to their shop for girls. Little princesses will be dazzled by the fairy-tale dresses, sparkly accessories, flowered flip-flops, and shiny slippers here. I found a pink wrap-style ballerina cardigan (£26) and a rose-print chiffon-over-satin dress (£44)—both reminiscent of dress-up clothes, sure to thrill a little girl. A great place for gifts, as children's clothing is not subject to VAT. The website has pictures of a few items.

ADDRESS
12 Long Acre
WC2 (Covent Garden or Leicester Square Tube)

PHONE
0207 836 1321

HOURS
Mon.–Fri. 10:00 a.m.–7:30 p.m.;
Sat. 10:00 a.m.–7:00 p.m.

WEBSITE
www.stanfords.co.uk
$

## 7  Stanford's
*Travel Bookshop*

If you find yourself in London without a proper guide, or you're traveling farther on from England and need direction, step into Stanford's and you'll be spoiled for choice. For 150 years, this big bookstore has offered an immense selection of travel guides, literature, maps, and phrase books, including hard-to-find volumes. Each country or region has its own separate section, so whatever your specific need, you'll have a choice of titles. While you're there, pick up a schedule of the Stanford-sponsored travel lectures at the Royal Geographical Society.

## 8   Coco de Mer

*Erotica*

"Delicious delights" is how this shop describes its high-class erotica. In front are racks of expensive, fetishy underthings (£90 is a typical price). In back is the more serious, but still-lighthearted, stuff. Be pleasantly shocked by the pillowcases that look like toile, but the scene is naughty, and there's a very naughty phrase cross-stitched on the back (£85). If that doesn't catch your fancy, perhaps the £520 leather corset or the beautiful books of erotica will. The shop was opened by Sammy Roddick, son of Body Shop founder Anita Roddick.

ADDRESS
23 Monmouth Street
WC2 (Covent Garden Tube)

PHONE
0207 836 8882

HOURS
Mon.–Sat. 11:30 a.m.–7:00 p.m.
(open Thurs. until 8:00 p.m.)
$$

## 9   The Loft

*Secondhand Designer Clothing*

The Loft is one of London's many secondhand designer clothing shops. Most of the wares seem nearly new, and the sizes are mostly very small, so it's easy to believe the shop's claim that the clothes have seen action only on the catwalk and in photo shoots. If you can fit into these diminutive sizes, you might find a gray Calvin Klein suit for £75, a pair of Moschino high-heeled mules for £44, Prada black patent-leather pumps still in

ADDRESS
35 Monmouth Street
WC2 (Covent Garden Tube)

PHONE
0207 240 3807

HOURS
Mon.–Sat. 11:00 a.m.–6:00 p.m.;
Sun. 1:00 p.m.–5:00 p.m.

WEBSITE
www.the-loft.co.uk
$

the box for £125, a Ronit Zilkha beige skirt suit for £44, or a DKNY long black sweater for £29. Men's is upstairs; women's is downstairs. There's a tiny sampling of items on their website.

## 10   ScreenFace
*Theatrical Makeup and Supplies*

ADDRESS
48 Monmouth Street
WC2 (Leicester Square or Covent Garden Tube)

PHONE
0207 836 3955

HOURS
Mon.–Sat. 10:00 a.m.–7:00 p.m.;
Sun. 12:00 p.m.–5:00 p.m.

WEBSITE
www.screenface.com

$

ScreenFace supplies professional cosmetics to the theater, television, and film industries, and it is open to the public. For makeup devotees, this place is like a big candy store, offering many lines of both professional-grade and consumer makeup and skincare products. There are also professional-quality special effects kits, body jewelry, hair products, and prosthetics. There is plenty of fun for the general shopper, too, with lots to tempt you or inspire your creativity: body jewelry, henna kits, beauty marks, tattoo stencils, facial jewelry. The website gives an idea of the enormous selection here.

This location is a branch. The main store, which is larger, is at 20–24 Powis Terrace, Westbourne Park Road, Notting Hill W11 (phone: 0207 221 8289).

## 11   Base Fashions
*Larger-Size Women's Fashions*

ADDRESS
55 Monmouth Street
WC2 (Leicester Square or Covent Garden Tube)

PHONE
0207 240 8914

HOURS
Mon.–Sat. 10:00 a.m.–6:00 p.m.

WEBSITE
www.base-fashions.co.uk

$$

Owner Rushka Murganovic spent twenty years in the fashion industry before opening her own shop specializing in sizes 18 and over. But she never asks your size. "I tell my customers to leave the size to me," she says. She and her staff fit customers in a clothing style Murganovic calls "central London with a kink." The store offers pretty blouses, handsome jackets, and quality suits with coordinating necklaces. "I give a larger-size figure something she can't find on the High Street," says Murganovic. You can preview a portion of the collection online.

## 12 Dress Circle

*Theater and Performance Soundtracks, Videos, Posters, Sheet Music*

Overhearing the conversations and casual chat in here tells you it's more than a store—it's practically a social club for people who love musical theater.

Dress Circle offers an enthusiast's selection of videos of plays, musicals, and performances in both the European PAL and American NTSC formats, and DVDs. You can find the sheet music to your favorite show, libretti from your favorite operas, show posters, CDs, karaoke tapes, and T-shirts.

The store also sponsors theater and other performances, and lists events of interest to theater fans on its website, which is updated often. Recently the shop has also put together theater outings that include reduced-price tickets and a pre-theater reception at the shop.

ADDRESS
57–59 Monmouth
WC2 (Leicester Square or Covent Garden Tube)

PHONE
0207 240 2227

HOURS
Mon.–Sat. 10:00 a.m.–6:30 p.m.
$–$$

ADDRESS
65 Monmouth Street
WC2 (Covent Garden or Leicester
Square Tube)

PHONE
0207 240 4280

HOURS
Mon.–Sat. 10:30 a.m.–6:30 p.m.;
Sun. 11:00 a.m.–6:30 p.m.
$$–$$$

## 13 Koh Samui
*Men's and Women's Clothing, Shoes*

Named after the idyllic Thai island, this sleek, minimal-ist boutique has a good assortment of designer clothing for the beautiful, rich, youthful, and thin. Koh Samui is perhaps best known as a champion of young British designers, reason enough to step in for a browse. They also carry Balenciaga street wear and club wear (which are a long way from your grandmother's Balenciaga) and own-label clothing. There are occasional markdowns and some wildly expensive items: a Koh Samui cardigan, £290; slip dress in polished cotton, £299.

ADDRESS
21A Tower Street
WC2 (Leicester Square Tube)

PHONE
0207 240 0931

HOURS
Mon. 1:00 p.m.–6:00 p.m.;
Tues.–Fri. 10:30 a.m.–6:00 p.m.;
Sat. 11:30 a.m.–5:00 p.m.
$

## 14 The Bead Shop
*Beads*

Queues form before the doors open at this little specialty shop, a part of the Beadworks network. Beadworks has a few U.S. outlets, primarily in the Northeast, but prices are lower in London. Table after table of box after box of sparkly, oblong, matte, multicolored, glazed, carved, iri-descent, teensy, and huge beads. Plenty of handmade and hand-painted beads, too. You could spend hours here, sifting through treasures for a sewing or jewelry-making project. Upstairs is retail; downstairs is wholesale.

# 15  Space.NK

*Beauty Products*

Space.NK was begun by Nicky Kinnaird, an aromatherapist who bases her formulations on aromatherapy and color therapy. The many London branches of Space.NK are a testimony to the popularity of her scrubs, salts, moisturizers, soaps, massage oils, and bath gels. If you need a little pampering, maybe one of her lovingly produced products, including home fragrances, will be just right.

The store carries other specialty skin lines, including REN (all the rage in Britain at this moment), Stila, Kiehls, Aesop, Cashmere Beauty, Eve Lom, and two lines of luxury products for men. Be aware that some of these are U.S. cult brands and cost less in the States. You'll find plenty of nice treats for £25 or less, including body lotion (from £12), massage oil (from £25), and shower wash (from £16).

ADDRESS
4 Thomas Neal's Yard
Earlham Street
WC2

PHONE
0207 379 7030

HOURS
Mon.–Sat. 10:00 a.m.–6:00 p.m.
(open Thurs. until 7:00 p.m.);
Sun. 12:00 p.m.–5:00 p.m.
$

BRANCHES:

(Within Harvey Nichols)
Knightsbridge
SW1

PHONE
0207 201 8636

KNIGHTSBRIDGE
307 Brompton Road
SW3

PHONE
0207 589 8250

CHELSEA
307 Kings Road
SW3

PHONE
0207 351 7209

KINGS ROAD
27 Duke of York Square
SW3

PHONE
0207 730 9841

MAYFAIR
45–47 Brook Street
W1

PHONE
0207 355 1727

MARYLEBONE
83a Marylebone High Street
W1

PHONE
0207 486 8791

DAY SPA
127–131 Westbourne Grove,
Notting Hill
W2

PHONE
0207 727 8063

KENSINGTON
3 Kensington Church Street
W8

PHONE
0207 376 2870

ADDRESS
16 Neal Street
WC2 (Covent Garden Tube)

PHONE
0207 240 0105

HOURS
Mon.–Sat. 10:00 a.m.–6:30 p.m.;
Sun. 1:00 p.m.–5:00 p.m.

WEBSITE
www.roughtrade.com

$

## 16 Rough Trade

*CDs and Vinyl Records*

Not the publishing and distributing powerhouse it once was, Rough Trade is still a magnet for the unusual and cutting edge in music. There's always something fantastic/annoying/captivating playing over the sound system, and the staff is enthusiastic about informing and assisting. Visit the website for inspiration. This shop is in the basement of Slam City Skates and is a branch of the main store in Notting Hill (*see page 193*).

ADDRESS
48 Neal Street
WC2 (Covent Garden Tube)

PHONE
0207 836 1666

HOURS
Mon.–Fri. 10:00 a.m.–6:00 p.m.
(open Thurs. until 7:00 p.m. from
April to December);
Sat. 10:30 a.m.–6:00 p.m.

$

## 17 The Kite Store

*Kites and Flying Toys*

Like the name says, this shop has kites and flying toys of every description. The most popular kite is the Flexifoil, but if you're inspired to make your own, they offer kite construction materials, including ripstop, and shafts from plain wooden rods to carbon. They also have kite-surfing and kite-buggy rigs (and can show you where to sign up for lessons and outings) and powerkites.

## 18   The Duffer of St. George
*Men's Clothing*

Just hip clothes, refreshingly without the pretentious décor common in such places. Male hipsters will return to the States a year ahead of fashion in designer casual and street wear, colorful shirts, and some dressy clothes in styles mostly tame enough to wear to the American workplace, if you're not a lawyer or investment banker. Everything looks as though Noel and Liam Gallagher of the rock band Oasis would wear it. The Duffer also offers its own-label sporty and dressy wear for clubbing and looking flash.

ADDRESS
29 and 34 Shorts Gardens
WC2 (Covent Garden Tube)

PHONE
0207 379 4660

HOURS
Mon.–Sat. 10:30 a.m.–7:00 p.m.;
Sun. 12:00 p.m.–5:00 p.m.
$$

## 19   Neal's Yard Dairy
*British Cheeses*

For two decades, a trip to London for many Brits has included a stop at Neal's Yard Dairy for its comprehensive selection of small-scale, farm-made cheeses that are ripened on-site. The shop is now possibly Britain's largest and certainly its most famous purveyor of artisanal cheeses. The store stocks real Cheshire cheeses, regional Stiltons, double Gloucesters, Shropshire blue, and Irish caerphilly among two hundred varieties. Sampling here is fun and educational, but what I always buy is Teifi, from Wales.

There's a deep selection of sheep's-milk cheeses, and a clear preference for cheeses made with unpasteurized

ADDRESS
19 Shorts Gardens
WC2 (Covent Garden Tube)

PHONE
0207 240 5700 (or for mail orders: 0207 645 3555)

HOURS
Mon.–Sat.10:00 a.m.–6:30 p.m.

E-MAIL
mailorder@nealsyarddairy.co.uk
$

milk. Here's your chance to sample a bigger selection of these types of cheese than can be found in the United States. You can see if you agree with the U.S. Food and Drug Administration that they should be banned for public health reasons.

The staff know the cheeses very well, and the salespeople are very good at helping you figure out your preferences. On a nice day, take your purchase out to the market square and eat it while you watch the street performers.

## 20   Paul Smith

*Men's, Women's, and Children's Fashion*

ADDRESS
40–44 Floral Street
WC2 (Covent Garden Tube)

PHONE
0207 379 7133

HOURS
Mon.–Fri. 10:30 a.m.–6:30 p.m.;
Sat. 10:00 a.m.–6:30 p.m.;
Sun. 1:00 p.m.–5:00 p.m.

WEBSITE
www.paulsmith.co.uk

Designer Paul Smith was knighted in 2001 for his service to the British fashion industry, and his sense of style is undeniable. His clothing for men, women, and children manages to be traditional but quirky, and, in most cases, wearable. Men with a sense of playful style might love the swinging London-styled jacket in brown with subtle orange and gray stripes (£795), or a traditionally cut but hippie-inspired patchwork shirt (£149).

Whatever you choose, everything from jeans (around £79) and T-shirts (both at the shop around the corner on Langley Court) to jackets and shoes is well designed.

And the items often incorporate surprising details: a nude cutie on the instep of a man's shoe, a skirt made of men's ties, cuff links styled like old typewriter keys. The website has very good photos of the current collections as well as archives of the old collections. The Paul Smith sale shop (23 Avery Row, W1) carries discontinued lines.

## 21 L. K. Bennett

*Women's Clothing and Shoes*

In Covent Garden, every store can seem to cater to twig-thin twenty-five-year-olds with deep, deep pockets. L. K. Bennett offers an alternative with racks of pretty and stylish shoes and ladylike suits, along with dresses and separates suitable for weddings, parties, or religious events. These are grouped by color and shown with matching scarves, shoes, and bags. If this style appeals to you, L. K. Bennett could be the kind of store you return to again and again. A matching shift-type sleeveless dress and coat in a nubby weave: £129 for the dress, £229 for the coat. L. K. Bennett is a top choice for shoe shopping among London's women professionals.

ADDRESS
130 Long Acre
WC2

PHONE
0207 379 1710

HOURS
Mon.–Fri. 10:30 a.m.–7:30 p.m.;
Sat. 10:00 a.m.–7:30 p.m.;
Sun. 11:00 a.m.–6:00 p.m.

BRANCHES
(Besides these, there are many suburban branches and one in the City of London.)

(WITHIN SELFRIDGE'S)
400 Oxford Street
W1C

PHONE
0207 318 2485

MAYFAIR
31 Brook Street
W1K (Bond Street Tube)

PHONE
0207 491 3005

CHELSEA
97 Kings Road
SW3 (Sloane Square Tube)

PHONE
0207 351 1231

KINGS ROAD
239 Kings Road
SW3 (Sloane Square Tube, then bus 11, 19, or 22)

PHONE
0207 376 7241

KENSINGTON
1 Kensington Church Street
W8 (Kensington High Street Tube)

PHONE
0207 937 6895

# WHERE TO EAT

## Amphitheatre Deli

ADDRESS
(within Royal Opera House)
WC2

PHONE
0207 212 9254

HOURS
Open for coffee and pastries, 10:00 a.m.–3:30 p.m.; for sandwiches, 11:30 a.m.–3:00 p.m.

People come to the Amphitheatre Deli, at the top of the escalators inside the Royal Opera House, just to take photos of the sweeping views of the building's interior. The deli's location above the main lobby gives it an extraordinary overlook of the opera house's glass walls and majestic vaulting. Have coffee and a pastry, or one of the limited, but very good, selection of sandwiches from £3.25 (cheddar and red onion relish) to £4.95 (Loch Fyne smoked salmon and lemon créme fraîche). Wine and champagne are served. It's an oasis from hectic Covent Garden, and the bathrooms are vast and spotless. (Note: Though the address is on Bow Street, it's more convenient to use the Covent Garden market square entrance.)

There is also the Amphitheatre Restaurant at this level, for a more formal dining experience. Visit www .royaloperahouse.org and click "your visit" for details. Telephone same as above.

# World Food Café

This small, casual eatery upstairs in Neal's Yard serves fresh, homemade vegetarian cooking. Each day there are three or four hot offerings, such as bean burritos, Sri Lankan thali, or Indian curried vegetables, as well as a menu of regular offerings such as falafel and Greek salads. The kitchen is a stove and work area surrounded by the counter where customers sit. Pull up to the U-shaped counter and watch as the servers dish up your meal from pots on the stove. Three smallish communal tables overlook Neal's Yard. Hot meals, £5.95 to £6.95.

ADDRESS
14 Neal's Yard (upstairs)
WC2

PHONE
0207 379 0298

HOURS
Mon.–Sat. 11:30 a.m.–4:30 p.m. (open Sat. until 5:00 p.m.)

# Belgo Centraal

The industrial entrance is stylishly spare and looks deceptively bare, because the action is all downstairs, where noisy communal tables seat Londoners scarfing down double-fried dutch fries, mussels every way, steak frites, roast chicken, belgian waffles, and brilliant specials. There is a big selection of Belgian, Dutch, and other Lowland beers. Great food, low prices, indestructible surroundings, and a fun atmosphere make Belgo a good choice for families. The best lunch deal is the express lunch at about £6, but even ordering à la carte will only set you back about £10 with beer.

ADDRESS
(entrances at 29 B Shelton Street and 50 Earlham Street)
WC2

PHONE
0207 813 2233

# Orso

A gem of a restaurant, offering Italian food that varies from good to very good at modest prices (for London). Starters like braised octopus and potato salad with black olives and red onions (£8), or warm baby artichokes with broad beans, lemon, and mint (£8) are fresh and authentic. Pastas are sold as smaller "first course" sizes and include flat noodles with pot-roasted oxtail and porcini, or ravioli of goat cheese and shallot with roasted garlic tomato sauce (both £8.50). Winning

ADDRESS
27 Wellington Street
WC2

PHONE
0207 240 5269

entrées such as crispy roast pork (£14) and roast sea bass (£17.50) are deftly executed at moderate prices. An even better value is the pre-theater menu, which is limited to two or three choices and served early and quickly, at a lower price than the full menu.

Children are welcome. Reservations recommended.

## Christopher's

ADDRESS
18 Wellington Street
WC2

PHONE
0207 240 4222

HOURS
Mon.–Fri. 12:00–3:00 p.m.;
5:00 p.m.–12:00 a.m.
Sat. 11:30 a.m.–4:00 p.m.;
5:00 p.m.–12:00 a.m.
Sun. 11:30 a.m.–4:00 p.m.

WEBSITE
www.christophersgrill.com

Up the sweeping staircase is a big, American-style grill offering a seasonal menu with the likes of roast chicken, crab cakes, clam chowder, Caesar salad, fine-quality steaks, lobster, and roast grouse. The wine list draws the admiration of the cognoscenti. Sunday brunch features eggs Benedict and scrambled eggs with salmon, all delivered by excellent servers.

Prices are high: With coffee and wine, you can expect to pay about £40 per person for two courses. The theater menu is a better value at two courses for £14.50 and three for £18.50.

Reservations are advisable. See a sample menu on the website.

## The Lamb & Flag

ADDRESS
33 Rose Street
(a little alley between Garrick Lane and Floral Street)
WC2 (Covent Garden or Leicester Square Tube)

PHONE
0207 497 9504

HOURS
Mon.–Thurs. 11:00 a.m.–11:00 p.m.; Fri.–Sat. 11:00 a.m.–10:45 p.m.; Sun. 12:00 p.m.–10:30 p.m.

The Lamb & Flag, Covent Garden's oldest pub at about three hundred years, is a lively and atmospheric place. If the crowded and smoky downstairs doesn't draw you, try the upstairs (with a restaurant). It's only lightly touristed, but some Londoners think it's the city's best pub. Well located for navigating Covent Garden, it's a good spot to arrange to meet someone, but since it's tucked away, you'll have to have a map, or ask on the street. (Note: No credit cards accepted.)

## Lowlander

Stop in for one of fourteen Lowland (Belgium and Holland) beers on tap plus thirty bottled varieties. Bitteballen (fried beef balls) and bittergarnituur, traditional Dutch and Belgian snacks, are available. Check the daily prix fixe menu, offering two courses for around £12. Children welcome.

ADDRESS
36 Drury Lane
WC2
PHONE
0207 79 7446

## Savoy

If you plan to have afternoon tea at one of London's grand hotels, the luxurious Savoy is a good choice. Proper little cucumber and smoked salmon sandwiches, scones with clotted cream, pastries, and hot tea in beautiful surroundings are brought to you by pampering servers. There's a "smart dress" code that bans tennis shoes and jeans, but you'll also feel underdressed in shorts and sandals. A reservation is a good idea. Prices: Mon.–Fri. £23 per person; Sat.–Sun. £26 per person.

ADDRESS
Strand
WC2
PHONE
0207 836 4343
HOURS
Teatime: 3:00 p.m.–5:30 p.m.

# CULTURE ALONG THE WAY

## Photographer's Gallery

Photographer's Gallery is one of England's premier venues for contemporary professional photography. The two galleries are a few doors away from each other and feature changing exhibitions. Admission to the gallery is free, and the galleries are compact enough to see everything quickly. Photo collectors will be interested in the sales room at Number 5, offering original and vintage photographic prints. Number 5 also has a little café in the back room where you can rest your feet and have a pastry. (There's a handy bathroom in the Number 5 gallery.)

ADDRESS
5 and 8 Great Newport Street
WC2 (Leicester Square Tube)
PHONE
0207 831 1772
HOURS
Mon.–Sat. 11:00 a.m.–6:00 p.m.;
Sun. 12:00 p.m.–6:00 p.m.

If you use little Langley Court to cut through from Long Acre to Shelton Street, you'll pass Pineapple Dance Studios. A window on the studio lets you peek in and take in a bit of jazz, tap, or salsa rehearsal. Next door is Pineapple's clothing shop, which sells fashionable dance and other active wear.

ADDRESS
Tavistock Street (Note: Entrance is on Russell Street)
WC2 (Covent Garden Tube)

PHONE
0207 943 4700

HOURS
Tues.–Sun. 10:00 a.m.–6:00 p.m.

WEBSITE
www.theatremuseum.org

## The Theatre Museum

Another of London's fantastic, free museums, this one has something for the whole family. In the main gallery, follow the history of theater. Another gallery traces the production of Wind in the Willows, from script to stage. Elsewhere, take in costume exhibits, sets, scripts, portraits. Several times daily there is a theater makeup demonstration. Performance videos let you see snippets of great dramatic productions and ballets—these are good for entertaining children while you view nearby exhibits. There are also hands-on activities for children, which are detailed on the website.

ADDRESS
Covent Garden Piazza
WC2

PHONE
0207 379 6344 (Recorded information line: 0207 565 7299)

HOURS
Sat.–Thurs. 10:00 a.m.–6:00 p.m.;
Fri. 11:00 a.m.–6:00 p.m.

## Transport Museum

Some people go to the museum; others go to the shop. Brilliant for small and cheap but distinctly London gifts: Tube stop refrigerator magnets (£2.99), socks and slippers patterned with Tube maps (socks, £2.99), London street signs (Abbey Road, Buckingham Palace), double-decker bus snow globes. There are videos that should make little boys flip, such as driver's-eye views of many London bus routes. Some of these are in American video format, but be sure to ask.

# OXFORD AND REGENT STREETS

## OXFORD STREET

THOUGH MANY shoppers head directly for Oxford Street, the shopping here is ordinary and quite expensive, while the sidewalks are crowded at all times, and absolutely heaving on weekends and during holiday shopping. Most Americans experience sticker shock at the "moderate" prices, and shoppers over age thirty-five may feel left out.

Most Oxford Street retailers are common British chain stores offering trendy fashion and footwear that are available for less in the States. Another segment is bona fide American stores: Gap, Gap Kids, Sunglass Hut, Disney Store, Skechers, and Niketown. Still another segment to avoid is European brands widely available in the U.S.—Benetton, Swatch—unless you are very familiar with prices and find them lower in England.

Big British department stores also maintain a presence on Oxford Street: **Debenhams, John Lewis, British Home Store,** and the more upscale **Marks & Spencer.** The shopping here is about what you'd find in the U.S., but the prices much higher. (It must be said, however, that Marks & Spencer underwear is considered the best made and best fitting in Britain.)

Regularly interspersed with these are card shops, souvenir shops, chain eateries, and endless mobile-phone stores. Every few blocks, everything seems to repeat itself, until you think it's cartoon scenery passing by over and over in a loop.

> When Oxford Street is unbearably crowded but you really want to shop in British department and chain stores, try Kings Road or Kensington High Street. Both have an abundance of the shops listed above, and neither is as crowded as Oxford Street.

If you do intend to shop Oxford Street, concentrate on menswear (**Cecil Gee, Suits You**) and on shops offering distinctive wares, such as **House of Fraser** and **Selfridge's**. House of Fraser is a highly respected store group with a premium mix of items, and the Oxford Street store is the flagship. For a description of Selfridge's, see facing page. The reasonably priced and very popular Spanish retailer **Zara** (*see page 114*) has an Oxford Street branch, as does the cheap and cheerful **H&M** (*see page 111*). **Evans** offers midpriced fashion for larger sizes, while **Viyella** is a sophisticated, upscale women's store along the line of Talbot's.

Young and fashion-conscious shoppers may insist on a trip to Oxford Street to see what young Brits are wearing. Some of the shops on Oxford Street selling catwalk knockoffs and trendy fashions include **Jigsaw, Kookai, TopShop, Miss Selfridge, Aldo** shoes, **Shelley's** shoes, **Claire's, Wallis** (for grown-up women), **Ann Summers** (racy underthings), **River Island, New Look, Monsoon, Russell & Bromley** shoes, and **French Connection UK**. (The alarming anagram F.rench C.onnection U.K. T-shirts are a big hit with English youths looking to express themselves more graphically.)

## Oxford and Regent Streets Shopping Areas

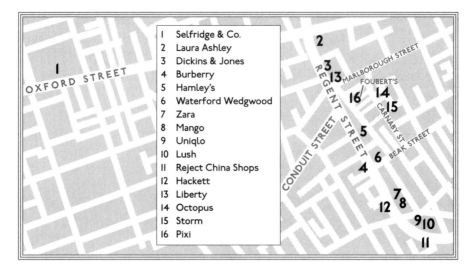

1  Selfridge & Co.
2  Laura Ashley
3  Dickins & Jones
4  Burberry
5  Hamley's
6  Waterford Wedgwood
7  Zara
8  Mango
9  Uniqlo
10 Lush
11 Reject China Shops
12 Hackett
13 Liberty
14 Octopus
15 Storm
16 Pixi

# 1 Selfridge & Co.

*Department Store*

ADDRESS
400 Oxford Street
W1A (Marble Arch or Bond
Street Tube)

PHONE
0870 837 7377

HOURS
Mon.–Fri. 10:00 a.m.–8:00 p.m.;
Sat. 9:30 a.m.–8:00 p.m.;
Sun. 12:00 p.m.–6:00 p.m.
$$–$$$

Many Brits feel this is the best department store in London and therefore the world. It's big, beautiful, and buzzy. Selfridge's has entirely adopted the "boutique" concept—each department is made up of separate boutiques: Instead of a book department, there's a little **W. H. Smith**'s; instead of a floral and garden department, there's a miniature **Jane Packer** shop; instead of a menswear department, there are **Thomas Pink, Dunhill, Duffer of St. George** (*see page 87*), and **Mulberry** boutiques. Add a standalone wine shop, a sweet shop, pen shop, tobacconist—and that's just the ground floor. It makes for a well-ordered shopping experience with the sensation of moving from store to store, absorbing a variety of what London retailers have to offer.

It's a brilliant strategy, with the advantages of efficiency and quality—you can shop all these stores under one roof. And you know what you're getting is the very finest quality. The only downside is that none of the boutiques is large enough to carry the designer's or manufacturer's full selection.

Especially fun are the boutiques for home décor and art, where you can eye the latest in glass décor; find clever, kid-size storage; see old familiars like **Alessi** and **Marimekko;** look through fine secondhand décor; shop for a Murphy bed; or browse in the **Halcyon** art gallery.

Weekends are a good time to visit Selfridge's, as the place is a hive of activity. On one visit, the sweet shop featured a chocolate fondue fountain, while in the children's department there was an hourly children's yoga demonstration. Over in cosmetics, artists turned the place into street performance as they used makeup to paint the bodies of young men.

# REGENT STREET

Like Oxford Street, Regent Street is heavy on British, American, and European chain stores selling merchandise available in the U.S.: Talbot's, Liz Claiborne, Benetton, Levi's, Church's shoes. However, there is fruitful shopping here, and many places mentioned in other chapters have Regent Street branches.

ADDRESS
256 Regent Street
W1B (Oxford Circus Tube)

PHONE
0207 437 9760

HOURS
Mon.–Fri. 10:00 a.m.–6:30 p.m.
(open Thurs. until 8:00 p.m.);
Sat. 9:30 a.m.–7:00 p.m.;
Sun. 12:00 p.m.–6:00 p.m.
$$

## 2   Laura Ashley
*Clothing, Home Furnishings*

Downstairs is clothing, and if you haven't shopped a Laura Ashley in a while, you'll be surprised at the sleek styles. Upstairs is a comprehensive range of home decorating fabrics, wallpapers, blinds, curtains, rugs, and furniture at prices lower than in the States.

ADDRESS
224 Regent Street
W1B (Oxford Circus Tube)

PHONE
0207 734 7070

HOURS
Mon.–Sat. 10:00 a.m.–7:00 p.m.
(open Thurs. until 8:00 p.m.); Sun.
10:00 a.m.–6:00 p.m.
$$–$$$

## 3   Dickins & Jones
*Department Store*

Dickins & Jones is a posh department store that features several floors of fashion and home décor items. The shop is really a collection of boutiques: **Hobbs, Ralph Lauren, Dolce & Gabbana, Versace, Nicole Farhi, Ted Baker.** The second floor houses an enormous shoe boutique with fashions from conservative to outlandish. There are also good menswear and evening wear departments.

---

### BRITISH SHOPPING HOURS

British stores typically close between 5:00 p.m. and 6:00 p.m., choosing one night of the week, usually Wednesday or Thursday, to remain open until 7:00 or even 8:00 p.m.

## 4    Burberry

*Fashion, Outerwear for Men, Women, and Youth*

The Burberry check is a fashion statement among street-savvy European youths, so you may find yourself making a mandatory excursion to the emporium of check. Every imaginable item of clothing is available in the distinctive pattern. Burberry has much more to offer these days—it has added extensive clothing lines by talented designers and is a full-blown purveyor of head-to-toe style. The New Bond Street store, opened in 2000, is the flagship.

BRANCHES:

MAYFAIR
21–23 New Bond Street
W1S (Bond Street Tube)
PHONE
0207 839 5222

KNIGHTSBRIDGE
2 Brompton Road
SW1 (Knightsbridge Tube)
PHONE
0207 581 2151

ADDRESS
165 Regent Street
W1B

PHONE
0207 734 4060

HOURS
Mon.–Sat. 10:00 a.m.–7:00 p.m.;
Sun. 12:00 p.m.–6:00 p.m.

## 5    Hamley's

*Toys*

The FAO Schwarz of London, Hamley's has been an institution since the eighteenth century. Hamley's is big, for England, with a thoughtful selection of the best toys spread over six floors: great dress-up clothes (get a plush crown, or a wizard's hat), an eye-popping array of Barbies, a delicious selection of craft and art kits, games, flying and wheeled toys, soft toys, and building kits. Assistants demonstrate the latest cool toys throughout the shop, and the bottom floor includes a video arcade, where you can skate on a virtual skateboard, drive a virtual eighteen-wheeler, dance on those weird dance machines, or explore other futuristic gaming options.

For the child who has everything and then some (and the parent even more), the whole store can be hired out for a sleepover birthday party.

ADDRESS
188–196 Regent Street
W1B (Oxford Circus Tube)

PHONE
0207 494 2000

HOURS
Mon.–Fri. 10:00 a.m.–8:00 p.m.;
Sat. 9:30 a.m.–8:00 p.m.;
Sun. 12:00 p.m.–6:00 p.m.
$–$$

ADDRESS
158 Regent Street
W1B

PHONE
0207 734 7262

## 6   Waterford Wedgwood

*(See page 33.)*

ADDRESS
120 Regent Street
W1B

PHONE
0207 851 4300

## 7   Zara

*(See page 114.)*

ADDRESS
106 Regent Street
W1B

PHONE
0207 434 1384

HOURS
Mon.–Sat. 10:00 a.m.–8:00 p.m.;
Sun. 12:00 p.m.–6:00 p.m.

## 8   Mango
*Fashion*

Like Zara, a successful Spanish fashion chain with low prices on trendy looks. More geared toward youth than Zara.

BRANCHES:

COVENT GARDEN
8–12 Neal Street
WC2H

PHONE
0207 240 6099

OXFORD STREET
225–235 Oxford Street
W1R

PHONE
0207 534 3505

ADDRESS
84–86 Regent Street
W1

PHONE
0207 434 9688

## 9   Uniqlo

*(See page 51.)*

ADDRESS
1 Quadrant Arcade, 82 Regent
Street
W1R

PHONE
0207 434 3953

## 10   Lush

*(See page 113.)*

## 11 Reject China Shops

*(See page 51.)*

## 12 Hackett

*(See page 37.)*

## 13 Liberty
*Department Store*

One block from Oxford Circus, where Regent Street meets Oxford Street, is the retail institution Liberty. The fabulous Tudor revival exterior is one of the most recognizable in the retail world. Inside, Liberty is beginning to show its age (about one hundred years) in the facility, and its history in the funny mix of merchandise—traditional home furnishings and up-to-the-minute fashions.

Liberty made its name on its home and dress fabrics, and it's still a destination for these. The furnishing fabrics departments carries traditional William Morris

ADDRESS
71 Regent Street
PHONE
0207 734 4915

ADDRESS
147 Regent Street
W1B
PHONE
0207 494 1855

ADDRESS
Regent Street at Great Marlborough Street
W1B (Oxford Circus Tube)
PHONE
0207 734 1234
HOURS
Mon.–Wed. 10:00 a.m.–6:30 p.m.;
Thurs. 10:00 a.m.–8:00 p.m.;
Fri.–Sat. 10:00 a.m.–7:00 p.m.;
Sun. 12:00 p.m.–6:00 p.m.
$–$$$
BRANCHES:

HEATHROW TERMINAL 3
Departures Airside
PHONE
0208 754 8488

HEATHROW TERMINAL 4
Departures Airside
PHONE
0208 754 1221

Arts & Crafts bolts (about £35 per meter), the Osborne & Little room (*see page 138*), and the Designers Guild fabrics (*see page 137*). The busiest room of all is devoted to Liberty's famous cotton lawn shirt and dress fabrics.

These seem a strange but charming holdover in a store that has elsewhere made a major push to update merchandise selections. The scarf department, for instance, is first-rate, fully modern, and packed with the most luscious scarves imaginable, including Liberty's own (about £39) and Georgina von Etzdorf's (*see page 33*). They also carry Lulu Guinness bags (*see page 68*).

Similarly, the jewelry department features case after case of ravishing artisanal and handmade jewelry, from funky to tribal to regal.

The women's wear department holds its own with a selection of designers not found everywhere else: Jennifer Dagworthy (for larger sizes), Eunwha, Ischiko, Dries van Noten, Chloe, Martine Sitbon, and the inimitable Annette Gortz.

# CARNABY STREET

WHEN YOU leave Liberty, ease down Carnaby Street, which has begun to revitalize after many years as a dreary tourist trap. Now there's a **Lush** (*see page 113*) , a **Muji** (*see page 115*), and other British high-street shops, plus a handful of independents.

## 14 Octopus
*Gifts*

For clever gifts and souvenirs on a budget, stop by Octopus. Everywhere in this tiny shop you'll find something loopy, like a gel-filled watchband (£6), or something useful, such as an unbreakable rubber vase (£18) or salt and pepper shakers on wheels (£8.50 each). Vibrant umbrellas, key chains, hologram handbags, funny bibs, picture frames, and lots of small items that might tempt young shoppers.

ADDRESS
28 Carnaby Street
W1F

PHONE
0207 287 3916

HOURS
Mon.–Sat. 10:00 a.m.–7:00 p.m.;
Sun. 12:00 p.m.–6:00 p.m.
$

BRANCHES:

COVENT GARDEN
54 Neal Street
WC2H (Covent Garden Tube)

PHONE
0207 836 2911

KINGS ROAD
130 Kings Road
SW3 (Sloane Square Tube)

PHONE
0207 589 1111

TROCADERO
13 Coventry Street
W1D (Piccadilly Circus Tube)

PHONE
0207 287 0988

 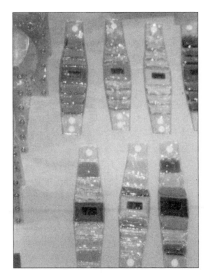

ADDRESS
21 Carnaby Street
W1F (Oxford Circus Tube)

PHONE
0207 437 1882

HOURS
Mon.–Sat. 10:00 a.m.–7:00 p.m.
(open Thurs. until 7:30 p.m.); Sun.
1:00 p.m.–6:00 p.m.
$

BRANCH:
37–39 Conway Street
W1T (Warren Street or Great
Portland Street Tube)

PHONE
0207 874 6902

## 15 Storm
*Watches, Jewelry*

Storm watches are so undeniably cool, it's worth at least window-shopping. They're sleek, innovative, modern steel and highly desirable at under £80. There's also a line of great-looking contemporary jewelry made from steel, polycarbonate, and semiprecious stones that looks like high-end designer pieces, but most are priced under £50.

ADDRESS
22A Fouberts Place
W1F (Oxford Circus Tube)

PHONE
0207 287 7211

HOURS
Mon.–Sat. 11:00 a.m.–7:00 p.m.;
Sun. 12:00 p.m.–5:00 p.m.
$

## 16 Pixi
*Cosmetics, Skincare Products*

Pixi was founded fairly recently by three gorgeous Swedish sisters, Petra, Sofia, and Sarah Strand, who look as if they don't need any makeup. Consequently, the emphasis is on light textures and sheer, natural colors. Pixi products are currently a favorite with cosmetics connoisseurs.

The shop is designed to look invitingly like a candy store, with bins and cubbies of products that just beg you to reach in and grab a handful. Playing and experimentation are encouraged, or if you want guidance, just ask. The skin cleansing cream is heavenly, the perfect balance of moisture and lightness. For young skin, there's a light cleansing gel (£16). Duo lip glosses (£14) and lip lacquers (£14) are fun, as is the eye/cheek/lip palette (£42). Cheek gels (£14) give a bit of glowing color to cheeks young and old without the painted-doll effect. This is a super stop for mothers and daughters, because both will find something here.

# WHERE TO EAT

Market Place, near the Oxford Circus tube, is a promising destination for an evening of bars, coffeehouses, restaurants, and excellent crowd-watching. Along James Street and in the courtyard at St. Christopher's Square, trattorias rub shoulders with an always-packed **Café Crêperie**, a family-friendly **Carluccio's** (delicious handmade pasta; *see page 42*), the reliable **Pizza Express**, as well as **Café Rouge** and **Starbucks**. There's a very clean public bathroom there, making this a handy stop when you're shopping Oxford Street.

**Selfridge's** has around twenty bars, cafés, and restaurants, including lunch places, coffee bars, a Yo! Sushi, a South American restaurant, juice bar, and fine dining. For variety and family-friendliness, try the Food Garden Café on the fourth floor. It's an all-under-one-roof concept: One cafeteria is divided into stations offering Lebanese food, Thai, crêpes, salad bar, British food, and espresso. Next door is a Häagen-Dazs.

## All Bar One

All Bar One is a reliably good chain of wine bars offering freshly made, modern European food in a casual setting for reasonable prices. Starters are less than £7, and entrées top out at around £10. It's technically a bar, not a restaurant, and children are not permitted. There are many branches of All Bar One in central London, including several in the City, two in Covent Garden, one each in Marylebone, Gloucester Road, Fulham Road, and Leicester Square, and many outside central London.

ADDRESS
289 Regent Street
W1R

PHONE
0207 467 9901

DINING HOURS:
12:00 p.m.–11:00 p.m.

## Mo

*(See page 42.)*

ADDRESS
23 Heddon Street
W1 (Oxford Circus Tube)

PHONE
0207 434 4040

HOURS
Mon.–Sat. 11:00 a.m.–11:00 p.m.

## Bodean's Barbeque

ADDRESS
10 Poland St.

PHONE
0207 287 7575

Hours
Mon.–Fri. 12:00–3:00 p.m.;
6:00–11:00 p.m.
Sat.–Sun. 12:00–11:00 p.m.

Bodean's is a double rarity in England—a kid-friendly restaurant and a vendor of passable pork and beef delicacies à la Texas, North Carolina, and points in between. Good value (for London): You can expect to pay £20 per person with drinks.

# CULTURE ALONG THE WAY

IF YOU'RE fortunate enough to be in London in early September, you may catch the Regent Street Festival, a performing arts festival of popular and classical music, theater, storytelling, and street entertainers, plus rides and special offers at area eateries.

## Trocadero

ADDRESS
13 Coventry Street
W1D (Piccadilly Circus Tube)

PHONE
0906 888 1100
0207 434 0034 (cinema)

HOURS
10:00 a.m.–1:00 a.m.

Visitors with older children and teens can plan an entertainment break at Trocadero just off Piccadilly Circus. This entertainment complex includes two video arcades with simulator rides, dodgem cars, a bowling alley, a pool room, stores that would interest young shoppers, and a cinema. Be aware that it's customary to book advance tickets for films. There's a branch of the cute and clever gift shop Octopus here (*see page 103 for full description*).

## The Wallace Collection

Behind Selfridge's a street or two in Manchester Square is the Wallace Collection of French furniture, porcelain, and paintings—all packed into a lavishly rehabilitated mansion. (*See page 186 for full description.*) There's a good restaurant, Café Bagatelle, on the premises.

# KENSINGTON

Perhaps because of its association with royalty and its convenient location near tourist attractions, Kensington Gardens, Hyde Park, Albert Hall, and premium shopping, Kensington is a very good choice for a stay. However, the area is expensive for real estate in general and hotels in particular. A studio apartment here sells for around £500,000. So there are few bargains to be found in hotels. However, South Kensington (really more to the east than to the south), in the neighborhood of the Natural History and Victoria & Albert Museums, does offer some reasonably priced accommodations.

Kensington High Street, though crowded, is a good alternative to the mob scene on Oxford Street for shopping British chain stores.

## WHERE TO STAY

### Gore Hotel

The Gore is highly eccentric, very jolly, and has an individual approach to hospitality. The interior is decorated with a collection of fifty-five hundred pieces of art. One suite is furnished with the first toilet designed by Thomas Crapper. And the Gore is reputed to possess a bed once owned by Judy Garland. Those are just an indication of the individual approach here.

Two Victorian mansions make up the hotel, and the owners have tried to maintain the character of the place by retaining decorative ceilings and architectural features.

ADDRESS
189 Queens Gate
SW7

PHONE
0207 584 6601

Recently, well-appointed meeting rooms and dining rooms were built in the lower ground floor.

The Gore is well situated between Kensington and Knightsbridge on Queens Gate, near Kensington High Street, Kensington Park, Victoria & Albert, and Harrods. The sole downside is that Queens Gate is home to many embassies, so nightlife is at a minimum. Still, the Gore has a hopping bar and a very good bistro. Rates: single, £155; double, £190; deluxe double, £285.

## John Howard Hotel

ADDRESS
4 Queens Gate
SW7

PHONE
0207 808 8400
0207 808 8401 (reservations)

Across Queens Gate from the Gore is the John Howard, a Best Western property. All the rooms are identically decorated in a predictable American 1980s hotel style, but the rates are competitive and the location is outstanding. The doubles are bigger than you'd expect in London, with all the amenities: satellite TV, trouser press, private bar, hair dryer, and air conditioning. The baths are spacious and modernized. There is a twenty-four-hour concierge, and the hotel has dining, banquet, and conference facilities. A single is £129; an executive single, £144; a standard double, £159; executive double, £169; and a junior suite, £189. Ask for a discount—

## TRANSPORTATION MATTERS

If you're staying in Kensington, Knightsbridge is quite close by. But taking the tube between them involves changing lines at South Kensington.

Instead, look for either the C1 or the number 52 bus, both of which run along Kensington Road to Knightsbridge. Catch the C1 anywhere on Kensington High Street or Kensington Road in front of the park. Catch the 52 anywhere on Kensington Church Street or Kensington Road. Both stop at the big five-way intersection in front of the Knightsbridge Tube station, a couple of blocks from Harrods.

The C1 also runs the other way, Knightsbridge to Kensington High Street, but takes the long way, going via Earl's Court. For a quicker ride, catch the number 9, 10, or 52 bus from the Knightsbridge Tube station.

they readily give them. They also have serviced apartments for longer stays.

## Milestone Hotel

Since even modest hotels in London cost an arm and a leg, you might as well get some luxury for your money. For about £250 a night, you can stay in the five-star Milestone, a hotel so discreet that many Londoners have never noticed it, though it fronts on Kensington Road.

The service starts before you arrive. You're asked to fill out a form indicating what music and newspapers you'd like in your room, and the temperature you'd like the room when you arrive. Exercise bike? Sure. Need a video? The reception desk has several. Shoes shined? Absolutely. Need voice mail in your native language? Okey-dokey. They even send up a staffer to demonstrate how to use the three remote controls for the television.

The rooms themselves are individually decorated and range from merely lovely to dazzling, with plenty of chintz and flounce, animal prints, and monstrous pieces of furniture. Beds are comfortable, with every shape and texture of pillow you could want. There are telephone extensions all over the place, including the bathroom, and broadband Internet access. Turndown service includes slippers and mineral water, plus a little inspirational book on your pillow and a scented candle burning in the bathroom. In the morning, the newspaper of your choice will be in a little bag hanging from your doorknob.

The Milestone houses the top-notch **Cheneston's** restaurant, which has a private dining room. The cozy lounge is a good place to doze off over a newspaper and a glass of brandy. The breakfasts are excellent. There's a small fitness center open twenty-four hours. It's the way to travel, even if just for a night or two.

Queen rooms, the smallest, start at £250 and range up to £305. A studio is £380; suites begin at £530. The Red Carnation group has several other four- and

ADDRESS
I Kensington Court
W8

PHONE
0207 917 1000

WEBSITE
www.redcarnationhotels.com

five-star hotels in central London. Visit their website for information.

## Vicarage Hotel

ADDRESS
10 Vicarage Gate
W8

PHONE
0207 229 4030

WEBSITE
www.londonvicaragehotel.com

The Vicarage is a real find for travelers who do not need a host of services but do want a clean, attractive, spacious room. This pretty bed-and-breakfast hotel is on a quiet street just off Kensington Church Street, about two blocks from Kensington High Street. The Vicarage offers big, bright rooms that are clean and pleasant, if not up-to-the-minute in décor. Rooms include hair dryers and ironing facilities.

Some rooms have private bath and toilet facilities, while others, much less expensive, share facilities European-style. There's a smallish lounge that people seem to love hanging around in, with TV and magazines.

There's no elevator in this multifloor hotel. Transactions are cash only, but prices are very attractive for the quiet, convenient location. A single with private facilities is £75; with shared facilities, £46. A double or twin with private facilities is £102; with shared facilities, £78. Triple rooms start at £95 with shared facilities. There are also quad rooms.

Vicarage Gate is actually two disconnected streets, so finding the hotel can be a little tricky. Ask for directions, or you'll spend twenty minutes wandering around Kensington.

# SHOPPING

## 1  Barker's

*Department Store*

This art deco wonder is a pretty average department store for London, which is to say there are nice designer things here and good makeup counters. There's not much reason to make a special trip, but the building is lovely, and as part of the prestigious House of Fraser chain, it's all the shopping some Londoners ever need.

ADDRESS
63 Kensington High Street
W8

PHONE
0207 937 5432

HOURS
Mon.–Fri. 10:00 a.m.–7:00 p.m.
(open Thurs. until 8:00 p.m.);
Sat. 9:30 a.m.–7:00 p.m.;
Sun. 12:00 p.m.–6:00 p.m.
$–$$$

## 2  H&M

*Clothing for Men, Women, and Children*

Also referred to affectionately as Hennes (the "H" of H&M), some Brits wonder why anyone shops anywhere besides this Swedish chain that sells trendy clothes at very low prices. Racks and racks of the latest looks are here, and teens and twenties in particular will be delighted.

H&M is also great for children's clothes. These are designed in seasonal suites like Gymboree's: Buy a matching dress, skirt, blouse, trousers, sweater, tights, and headband. The only drawback with H&M clothing is quality. Some items are well-made; others are not so durable. But they'll probably be out of style, out of season, or outgrown by the time they wear out anyway.

ADDRESS
103–111 Kensington High Street
W8

PHONE
0207 368 3920

HOURS
Mon.–Sat. 10:00 a.m.–7:00 p.m.
(open Thurs. until 8:00 p.m.); Sun.
12:00 p.m.–6:00 p.m.
$

BRANCHES:

REGENT STREET
261–271 Regent Street
W1 (Oxford Circus Tube)
PHONE
0207 493 4004

OXFORD STREET
481 Oxford Street
W1 (Marble Arch Tube)
PHONE
0207 493 8557

OXFORD STREET
360–366 Oxford Street
W1 (Oxford Circus or Marble Arch Tube)
PHONE
0207 518 1630

OXFORD STREET
174–176 Oxford Street
W1 (Oxford Circus or Marble Arch Tube)
PHONE
0207 612 1820

## 3 Trotters Childrenswear

*Children's Clothing, Hairdresser, Shoes*

ADDRESS

127 Kensington High Street

W8

PHONE

0207 937 9373

HOURS

Mon.–Fri. 10:00 a.m.–8:00 p.m.;

Sat. 9:00 a.m.–7:00 p.m.;

Sun. 10:30 a.m.–5:00 p.m.

$

BRANCH:

KINGS ROAD

34 Kings Road

SW3 (Sloane Square Tube)

PHONE

0207 259 9620

Just outside the Tube station, Trotters carries a choice assortment of children's play clothing, swimsuits, and pajamas. Fitting shoes is a specialty here, and children sit in the Trotters Express "bus" to be properly measured. Among the brands they carry are Stride Rite, called Start Rite in England, and Buckle My Shoe, another premium brand favored by English mums in the know. There's also a hairdresser available (£11.50 for an under-age-five haircut); kids are treated to a view inside the portholes of a rocket ship while they have their hair cut. There is also a small selection of high-quality toys.

## Kensington Shopping Area

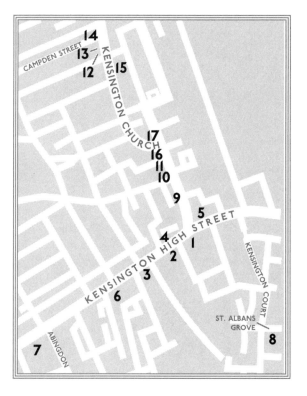

| | |
|---|---|
| 1 | Barker's |
| 2 | H&M |
| 3 | Trotters Childrenswear |
| 4 | Lush |
| 5 | Zara |
| 6 | Muji |
| 7 | Children's Book Centre |
| 8 | Raj Tent Club |
| 9 | Portmeirion |
| 10 | Designer Bargains |
| 11 | What Katy Did |
| 12 | Garry Atkins |
| 13 | Eila Grahame Antiques |
| 14 | Roderick Jellicoe |
| 15 | Brian Rolleston Antiques Ltd. |
| 16 | Raffety and Walwyn |
| 17 | Michael German Antiques |

# 4   Lush

*Handmade Bath Products and Toiletries*

You'll smell Lush before you see it, and when you've walked in, you'll think you're in a magical greengrocer's. The colorful mounds of homemade soap and bath bombs look and smell good enough to eat. The walls look like a wizard's apothecary, bulging with jars, tubes, and tubs of handmade organic creams, lotions, masks, balms, scrubs, powders, and deodorants. Barrels of ice hold perishable, freshly made facemasks and creams. This is my first stop, where I pick up the rose-scented, skin-smoothing Wow Wow mask (about £4).

Lush products are made from organic natural ingredients in appealing combinations. Little girls will love the fragrant, sparkly bath bombs and the candy-scented Angels Delight soap. Big girls will like the rose-scented lip balm (makes a great cuticle cream), the Strawberry Boat body scrub, the Butterball bath bomb (with cocoa butter bits that melt in the water), and the soothing, spiced Karma soap. Guys will like Cosmetic Lad, a moisturizer for freshly shaved faces. Parents will like no-spill bubble bars—just drop a slice under running water—and no-spill solid shampoo bars. You'll want one of everything in the store. And it's so cheap, you can probably afford it. See the product offerings on the website.

**ADDRESS**
96 Kensington High Street
W8

**PHONE**
0207 376 1970

**HOURS**
Mon.–Sat. 10:00 a.m.–7:00 p.m.;
Sun. 12:00 p.m.–7:00 p.m.

**WEBSITE**
www.lush.co.uk
$

BRANCHES:

LIVERPOOL STREET
STATION
(Unit 55 Broadgate Link)
EC2
PHONE
0207 247 6983

HEATHROW AIRPORT,
TERMINAL 3
TW6
PHONE
0208 759 5551

CHELSEA
123 Kings Road
SW3 (Sloane Square Tube)
PHONE
0207 376 8348

COVENT GARDEN
The Piazza
WC2E (Covent Garden Tube)
PHONE
0207 240 4570

SOHO
40 Carnaby Street
W1V (Oxford Circus Tube)
PHONE
0207 287 5874

REGENT STREET
80–82 Regent Street
W1R (Piccadilly Circus Tube)
PHONE
0207 434 393

ADDRESS
48–52 Kensington High Street
W8

PHONE
0207 368 4680

HOURS
Mon.–Sat. 10:00 a.m.–7:00 p.m.
(open Thurs. until 8:00 p.m.); Sun.
12:00 p.m.–6:00 p.m.

$

BRANCH:

REGENT STREET
120 Regent Street
W1 (Piccadilly Circus Tube)

PHONE
0207 851 4300

# 5   Zara

*Men's, Women's, and Children's Clothing*

This Spanish chain, along with Mango, has been a big success in England (and New York and Paris) by offering catwalk knockoffs at reasonable prices. If you're going to buy trendy clothing in London, this is your best bet, because the trendiness is dialed down a notch, and prices are low enough that you can make an impulse purchase and not have buyer's remorse the next day. And if you like what you bought, you're in luck, as Zara clothing holds up reasonably well.

Youths will be drawn to bare and up-to-the-minute looks. But there are also suits, blouses, and jeans for the not so young; stylish but not outrageous men's and young men's clothing; and cute children's clothing.

# 6 Muji

*Stylish Homewares and Office Supplies*

The thing that's so lovable about Muji is that it makes buying a spiral notebook seem so urban and minimalist. The store, a Japan-based chain begun in Tokyo in 1983, has a sleek, monochromatic look that you'll begin to think might look good in your house.

As for the product selection, if Restoration Hardware and Office Depot were to crash into Target in Tokyo, this is what might result. Stylish and inexpensive household, kitchen, and office items predominate, including storage, trash cans, chrome tissue-box covers, bath salts, tweezers, camp stools (£4.99), art supplies, tumblers (£2.50), binders and such. Muji is good for practical gifts, or for picking up a notebook or travel diary or binder for travel scraps.

Downstairs in some locations, including Covent Garden and Knightsbridge, is clothing, which is well designed and inexpensive, if very basic, and in minimalist colors—charcoal, khaki, black, brown. T-shirts around £15, in half a dozen colors; canvas jackets, £75; drawstring cotton trousers, £25.

ADDRESS
157 Kensington High Street
SW8
(Kensington High Street Tube)

PHONE
0207 376 2484

HOURS
Mon. 10:30 a.m.–7:00 p.m.;
Tue.–Sat. 10:00 a.m.–7:00 p.m.
(open Thurs.–Fri. until 7:30 p.m.);
Sun. 12:00 p.m.–6:00 p.m.
$–$$

BRANCHES:

SOHO
41 Carnaby Street
W1 (Oxford Circus Tube)
PHONE
0207 287 7323

COVENT GARDEN
135 Long Acre
Covent Garden
WC2 (Covent Garden Tube)
PHONE
0207 379 0820

TOTTENHAM COURT ROAD
6–17 Tottenham Court Road
W1 (Tottenham Court Road Tube)
PHONE
0207 436 1779

OXFORD STREET
187 Oxford Street
W1R (Oxford Circus Tube)
PHONE
0207 437 7503

(WITHIN SELFRIDGE'S)
400 Oxford Street
W1R (Marble Arch Tube)
PHONE
0207 318 3452

CHELSEA
118/118A Kings Road
SW3 (Sloane Square Tube)
PHONE
0207 823 8688

# 7   Children's Book Centre

*Books and Toys*

ADDRESS
237 Kensington High Street
W8 (Kensington High Street Tube.
The shop is some distance down
the street, so catch the number 9 or
10 bus.)

PHONE
0207 937 7497

HOURS
Mon.–Sat. 9:30 a.m.–6:30 p.m.
(open Thurs. until 7:00 p.m.);
Sun. 12:00 p.m.–6:00 p.m.
$

Travelers with young children should consider combining a visit to Children's Book Centre with a visit to Holland Park across the street. The busy, colorful front window is your cue that Children's Book Centre is a floor-to-ceiling book and toy treasury. The largest children's bookstore in London, it carries a thoughtful selection of children's literature and a fair amount of software and computer games as well, plus party supplies and greeting cards. Downstairs are toys, crafts (we loved the chocolate craft kit), games, puzzles, dolls, trucks, and tanks, all piled high.

## 8 Raj Tent Club

*Fantasy Party Tents*

For an exotic, romantic party tent you won't see anywhere else, visit Raj Tent Club on a little street behind
Kensington High Street (it's across the street from
Wodka [*see page 125*]). Designer Clarissa Mitchell
started her shop to re-create the opulent Moghal
hunting and picnic tents for a clientele that wants a
memorable party setting. Hers are lined, portable,
pole-supported tents. Pergolas, pavilions, canopies,
and beach tents are soft, muted shades of cream, gray,
and blue outside, while inside they are elaborately decorated with tiny mirrors, stars, prints, and gold stitch-
ing. The shop does a brisk business in travel as well as
party tents. Visit the website to see their fantasy cre-
ations. Prices start at £450 and go up and up for enormous tents with covered porches and blinds.

Raj Tent Club also has a small selection of Indian
decorative items such as pillows, dishes, and other
objects that make good gifts.

ADDRESS
14 St. Albans Grove
W8

PHONE
0207 376 9066

HOURS
Mon.–Fri 9:30 a.m.–5:30 p.m.;
Sat. by appointment only

WEBSITE
www.rajtentclub.com
$$–$$$$

# KENSINGTON CHURCH STREET

SPEND A morning on this little street off Kensington High Street near the Tube stop for promising shops, fine antiques, and good eateries. Kensington Church Street is best known as a destination for antique lovers. About eighty antique dealers are located along the road and its side streets. Of these, approximately twenty specialize in English, Continental, and Oriental pottery and porcelain, a bonanza for collectors.

ADDRESS
13 Kensington Church Street
W8

PHONE
0207 938 1891

HOURS
Mon.–Sat. 10:00 a.m.–6:00 p.m.
$–$$

## 9  Portmeirion

*Dishware*

Portmeirion's only retail outlet outside Stoke-on-Trent, this is actually a showroom with retail sales, and prices are generally lower than in the States. The selection here is deep—any Portmeirion you fancy is likely to be here (although a couple of patterns are available only in the U.S.). Besides the lower prices, you can reclaim VAT on purchases as small as £50.

ADDRESS
29 Kensington Church Street
W8

PHONE
0207 795 6777

HOURS
Mon.–Sat. 10:00 a.m.–6:00 p.m.
$–$$

## 10  Designer Bargains

*Women's Designer Clothing Reseller*

Since London fashion is a couple of years ahead of U.S. trends, you can shop the secondhand stores and bring home a sackful of looks that are "so last year" for London but the next big thing for the States. Designer Bargains offers packed racks of true designer clothing, some never worn, at prices lower than other resellers. Expect to find goodies like a Chanel sequined evening jacket, £420; a Moschino bright green long-sleeved knit top, £79; Jimmy Choo shoes, £150; and a Jasper Conran leather dress, £250.

You'll find even better values downstairs, where items are marked down to move. I once found a reversible red cashmere-and-silk-satin Valentino evening coat for £150, a fraction of what it would have cost new.

## 11 What Katy Did

*Children's Clothing*

Darling and expensive togs for the well-dressed tyke. A big hit in recent years were the onesies that read "I've just done 9 months inside" and "My daddy is rich and my mama's good looking." Also look for onesies in Scottish cashmere and Cookie-brand handmade outfits. Boys always seem to lose out in cute children's clothing, but here the selections for boys are especially funky and adorable. A darling pair of trousers goes for £43.99, and matching jacket, £75.99; girl's multicolored cotton cardigan, £56; jumper and T-shirt, £43.99; a cotton summer dress, £28.99.

ADDRESS
49 Kensington Church Street
W8 (Kensington High Street Tube)

PHONE
0207 937 6499

HOURS
Mon.–Sat. 10:30 a.m.–5:30 p.m.
$–$$

# ANTIQUES

## 12 Garry Atkins

Go, but don't take the kids, to Garry Atkins for two showrooms of English pottery, from medieval to eighteenth-century. Atkins says he has plenty of American customers—he attends the Armory Show in New York in January. To preview his collection, visit the website.

ADDRESS
107 Kensington Church Street
W8 (Notting Hill Gate Tube)

PHONE
0207 727 8737

WEBSITE
www.englishpottery.com

## 13 Eila Grahame Antiques

If you're more interested in *objets* than *armoires,* try Eila Grahame Antiques. Every time you glance around the shop, something different grabs your attention: a birdcage, an embossed-leather room screen, a decoupage fire screen, a pub sign, an oversize tankard—Grahame has an eye for the whimsical and decorative.

ADDRESS
97C Kensington Church Street
W8

PHONE
0207 727 4132

ADDRESS
3A Campden Street
(off Kensington Church Street)
W8 (Notting Hill Tube)

PHONE
0207 727 1571

WEBSITE
www.EnglishPorcelain.com

## 14   Roderick Jellicoe

Roderick Jellicoe specializes in eighteenth-century porcelain. Jellicoe and Atkins, along with neighboring ceramics dealers Simon Spero and Mercury Antiques, hold an annual show and sale that's worth finding out about if you're serious about English ceramics. The website has details and previews of products.

ADDRESS
104A Kensington Church Street
W8

PHONE
0207 729 5892

## 15   Brian Rolleston Antiques Ltd.

For authentically English, indisputably tasteful furnishings, try Brian Rolleston Antiques. For decades, this family-run firm has specialized in eighteenth- and early-nineteenth-century furniture, particularly walnut. Everything—gleaming mirrors, elegant dining tables, and graceful chairs—is in superb condition.

ADDRESS
79 Kensington Church Street
W8

PHONE
0207 938 1100

WEBSITE
www.raffetyantiqueclocks.com

## 16   Raffety and Walwyn

This establishment is best visited just before the hour, so you can hear the chiming of their antique clocks. Raffety and Walwyn has been acquiring and selling antique clocks for twenty years. The pieces, which date from the seventeenth to the nineteenth centuries, are original, high-quality, decorative, and guaranteed to be in working order. Clock prices range from about £5,000 to more than £30,000 for the finest and rarest. The shop will ship to U.S. addresses and provide detailed setup instructions. Have a look at current stock on their website.

# 17 Michael German Antiques

As owner Michael German says, a walking stick was the designer label of the times in Victorian England. Ladies and gentlemen had canes for day and night, for town and country, and more—the average "person of quality" owned more than ten walking sticks. London in 1900 was home to sixty cane shops, where patrons first chose the handle, then selected wood—brown for day, black for evening. Since canes have gone the way of all fashion, German's shop has been able to buy up hundreds of this one-time must-have. He also has a selection of antique weapons and armor. His websites show some of his stock.

ADDRESS
38B Kensington Church Street

PHONE
0207 937 2771

WEBSITES
www.antiquecanes.com
www.antiqueweapons.com

# WHERE TO EAT

## Clarke's

ADDRESS
124 Kensington Church Street
W8 (Notting Hill Gate Tube)

PHONE
0207 221 9225

HOURS
Lunch 12:00–2:00 p.m.
Dinner 7:00–10:00 p.m.

The menu in this pretty, intimate place is whatever inspiration chef/proprietor Sally Clarke has that day. Her California-influenced cooking draws on hand-raised an artisan ingredients such as local fish, Scottish seafood, and Italian ham. Expect menu choices of steak, grilled swordfish, roast breast of corn-fed chicken, and grilled Scottish scallops, with all the requisite frills like Parmesan shavings and truffles. There are always attractive salad selections, like roast duck leg salad, and clam and mussel salad with fennel and watercress.

At lunch you can choose from three main courses and several salads. The main courses are £14, and the salads, many of which are substantial enough to make a meal, are around £9. Dinner is a set menu of four courses for about £50.

The bread, baked by Clarke's bakery next door, is exceptionally good. And the desserts are simply amazing, from homemade ice creams to pistachio meringues with lemon curd cream. The wine list includes some reasonably priced bottles and good by-the-glass selections.

Reservations recommended. If Clarke's is not in the budget, treat yourself to . . .

## & Clarke

ADDRESS
122 Kensington Church Street
W8 (Notting Hill Gate Tube)

PHONE
0207 229 2190

Next to Clarke's is her bakery and deli, which offers dozens of bread varieties that Londoners rave over, plus tarts, pastries, pizzas, handmade chocolate truffles, butter-rich gingersnaps, and brownies.

## The Churchill Arms

You can have two experiences here in one visit, as the Churchill is a proper English pub up front, a Thai restaurant in back.

Start with a beer in the woody old English front of the building. It's usually crowded and smoky, even during the day.

Then wander back for very good, freshly cooked Thai food in satisfying portions. Some people feel it's among the best Thai food in London, and the prices are very reasonable. Understandably, the place is always crowded. You should reserve a table for dinner, but you might find one free at lunch. Lunch is around £6; dinner around £15.

ADDRESS
19 Kensington Church Street
(Notting Hill Gate Tube)

PHONE
0207 792 1246

HOURS
Mon.–Sat. 11:00 a.m.–11:00 p.m.;
Sun. 12–10:30 p.m.
Food served 12:00–2:30 p.m. and
6:00–9:30 p.m.

## Orangery

This three-hundred-year-old structure, built for Queen Anne to use as a greenhouse in winter and a ballroom in summer, likely looks much as it did in her time, except for the tables of casually dressed visitors. This soaring, regal space, decorated with Grinling Gibbons carvings (he also did the carvings in the church of St. James Piccadilly [see page 39]), is utterly delightful. Tuck into coffee and pastry, or something more substantial from the brief menu of very good salads, sandwiches, soups, and a few main courses. Pastries from £1.75; starters from £5.95; main courses from £6.95 to £8.95. Wine and beer are available. The Orangery can be crowded on the weekends, but you can usually get a table within a few minutes.

ADDRESS
Kensington Palace
(in Kensington Gardens)
W8 (Kensington High Street Tube)

PHONE
0207 376 0239

HOURS
Lunch 12:00 p.m.–3:00 p.m.; tea
after that until 6:00 p.m.

# Wagamama

ADDRESS
26 Kensington High Street
(Kensington High Street Tube)
PHONE
0207 376 1717

One of a London-wide chain of noodle shops offering generous, tasty bowls full of the likes of chili chicken ramen, katsu chicken curry, Thai shrimp curry over noodles, pork char siu on noodles, and lots of vegetarian options. Seating is at long communal tables, and the emphasis is on turnover, so it's not exactly a quiet dinner for two. The fresh juices are a treat, and wine, beer, and sake are available. Expect to spend £10 per person.

BRANCHES:

BLOOMSBURY
4A Streatham Street
WC1A
PHONE
0207 323 9223

MARYLEBONE
101A Wigmore Street
W1H
PHONE
0207 409 0111

COVENT GARDEN
Tavistock Street
WC2E
PHONE
0207 836 3330

SOHO
10A Lexington Street
W1R
PHONE
0207 292 0990

KNIGHTSBRIDGE
(lower ground floor of Harvey
Nichols)
109 Knightsbridge
SW1X
PHONE
0207 201 8000

LEICESTER SQUARE
14A Irving Street
WC1H
PHONE
0207 839 2323

# Wodka

This restaurant, tucked into the neighborhood behind Kensington High Street, has been around for twenty years serving fine Polish-inspired food, always with an expert hand and a light touch. Starters hover around £8 but range from £5 to £23 (for an osetra caviar blini) and include delights such as feather-light veal dumplings and tender pierogi.

Main courses include roast duck, beef goulash, paprika chicken, and red peppers stuffed with kasha and feta—all twists on Polish classics. Most are priced under £18.

Wodka maintains its neighborhood regulars with a selection of non-Polish *plats du jour,* all appealing and expertly cooked.

The prices are very reasonable, unless you dip into the long and alluring list of vodkas. These are classified by flavor profile: dry and clear; sweet and spicy, etc. With so many temptations, at £2.25 to £2.75 per shot, you could do a lot of damage.

The nicest thing about Wodka is that since it isn't the hot place of the moment, you can usually get in without a reservation.

ADDRESS
12 St. Albans Grove
W8 (Kensington High Street Tube)

PHONE
0207 937 6513

HOURS
Mon.–Fri. 12:30–2:30 p.m.;
7:00–11:15 p.m.;
Sat.–Sun. 7:00–11:15 p.m.

# CULTURE ALONG THE WAY

FANS OF British comic Benny Hill may wish to pass his former residence and doff their caps. Hill lived at 1 and 2 Queens Gate Street from 1960 to 1986. The home is privately owned, but the Dead Comics Society has placed a plaque on the house to mark it.

ADDRESS
2–24 Kensington High Street

PHONE
0207 361 1910

HOURS (BAR):
Mon.–Fri. 12:00 p.m.–2:30 p.m.;
Sat. 5:30 p.m.–11:00 p.m.

## The Tenth at Royal Garden Hotel

The Royal Garden Hotel is unprepossessing from the street but has a tenth-floor bar, the Tenth, that has fantastic views over Kensington Gardens and Hyde Park. Take the elevator to the top floor for a late afternoon drink.

## Kensington Gardens

Kensington Gardens is a vast, open park with lots to do. Tour Kensington Palace, take the children to the secure and fantastically entertaining Diana Princess of Wales Memorial Playground, take in contemporary art in the Serpentine Gallery, or just amble around the extensive paths. The public toilet in the park, right on Kensington Road, is handy to know about.

The broad, paved paths of Kensington Gardens are an excellent skating surface; rent skates from Slick Willie's, 41 Kensington High Street (phone: 0207 937 3824).

# KINGS ROAD

*I*N ITS OWN WAY, Kings Road is as fertile a shopping ground as Bond Street. Certainly it has more shops with down-to-earth prices, and despite the arrival of several chain stores, many Kings Road stores are individually owned and operated, with a personal selection of merchandise and committed service.

There's so much more on Kings Road than what space here will allow—you deserve to spend a day or two shopping the area and making your own discoveries.

## WHERE TO STAY

### Sloane Hotel

The Sloane is a quiet twenty-two-room boutique hotel set among grand townhomes on a residential street one block off Kings Road. The hotel is prettily decorated with good furniture, some antiques, and fine fabrics. Each of the fairly lavish rooms is individually furnished with heavy curtains, deluxe beds, and antique pieces that are for sale (inquire at the reception desk).

The amenities are better than average—air conditioning, Internet access, voice mail, secretarial services, translation. There's tea when you need it, twenty-four-hour room service (English breakfast, £12), laundry, concierge, and various other services.

The Sloane's location is good for shopping Kings Road, Sloane Square, and Sloane Street (*page 69*). A

ADDRESS
29 Draycott Place
SW3

PHONE
0207 581 5757 in England;
toll-free in the U.S. 800-324-9960

WEBSITE
www.sloanehotel.com

short walk away are Walton/Beauchamp/Pont Streets (*see pages 55–59*), and Fulham Road is within striking distance. Harvey Nichols and Harrods are a fifteen-minute walk, or one Tube stop away.

The only drawback to the otherwise terrific location is that the city's major tourist attractions are not especially nearby. If that's what you came to London for, you may want a more central location, such as Kensington, Covent Garden, or Regent Street.

Singles are available from £165; doubles from £185. Haggle and they might knock a bit off the prices.

## SHOPPING

Most people enter Kings Road from the Sloane Square Tube station. At Sloane Square you'll find Peter Jones, the hardworking department store of modest ambitions (*see page 62*), and a clientele that's a grand cross section of London's populace.

Past Peter Jones is a branch of **Trotter's** children's shop at 34 Kings Road (*see page 112*). Across Symons Street from Peter Jones is **General Trading Company,** an expensive lifestyle department store offering tabletop, furniture, and décor items. Londoners shop here for the latest home looks. A visit may get your creative juices flowing, but you'll find it for less in the States.

The very top section of Kings Road near the Sloane Square Tube stop features mostly designer fashion: **Ronit Zilkha**'s fun clothes and **iBlues,** which is the more formal range of **MaxMara,** are among the shops.

### GETTING AROUND KINGS ROAD

Kings Road is very long, and Sloane Square is the sole Tube stop. Your feet will be tired long before you've reached all the shops on your list, so plan to take the bus. The numbers 11, 19, and 22 buses all run along Kings Road, each one several times an hour.

Across Kings Road from Trotter's is **Duke of York Square,** opened in spring 2003. This revamped square was once the Duke of York's military headquarters. It now includes apartments, office space, cafés, and lots of smallish and midsize shops. So far, the trend is toward quality women's wear, but there are several other interesting shops opening, including a branch of the shop **Space.NK** (*see page 85*).

At the back of the square is an outpost of **Patisserie Valerie,** which is always good for brunch, tea, or a sandwich or scone to go.

As you move down Kings Road toward Jubilee Place, you'll find common British high-street shops such as **Marks & Spencer, Oasis, Next, Muji, Warehouse,** and **French Connection.** Kings Road is a good alternative to the jam-packed sidewalks of Oxford Street for shopping the big British names.

## Kings Road Shopping Area

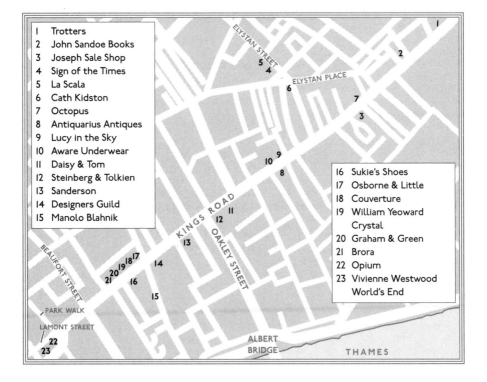

1  Trotters
2  John Sandoe Books
3  Joseph Sale Shop
4  Sign of the Times
5  La Scala
6  Cath Kidston
7  Octopus
8  Antiquarius Antiques
9  Lucy in the Sky
10 Aware Underwear
11 Daisy & Tom
12 Steinberg & Tolkien
13 Sanderson
14 Designers Guild
15 Manolo Blahnik

16 Sukie's Shoes
17 Osborne & Little
18 Couverture
19 William Yeoward Crystal
20 Graham & Green
21 Brora
22 Opium
23 Vivienne Westwood World's End

ADDRESS
34 Kings Road
SW3

PHONE
0207 259 9620

ADDRESS
10 Blacklands Terrace
SW3

PHONE
0207 589 9473

HOURS
Mon.–Sat. 9:30 a.m.–5:30 p.m.
(open Wed. until 7:30 p.m.)

WEBSITE
www.johnsandoe.com
$

## 1 Trotters
*Children's Clothing, Accessories, Shoes, and Hair Salon*

(*See page 112.*)

## 2 John Sandoe Books
*Books*

Just off the corner of Kings Road, two blocks from Sloane Square, is this little shop, a thousand square feet on three floors, crammed floor-to-ceiling with not-your-average selection of books. They have an enormous number of titles but only a copy or two of each. It looks like a hodgepodge to the untrained eye, but the helpful partners know exactly where to go to find what you're looking for.

The shop publishes a quarterly list of upcoming titles that serves as a catalog. You can order from the list or use it as a reminder of when a favorite book is due to be released.

John Sandoe is the kind of bookstore that inspires loyalty. It was recently included in the book *Trading Places: Europe's Finest Specialty Shops.*

ADDRESS
53 Kings Road
SW3

PHONE
0207 730 7562

HOURS
Mon.–Sat. 10:00 a.m.–6:30 p.m.
(open Wed. until 7:00 p.m.);
Sun. 1:00 p.m.–6:00 p.m.
$–$$

## 3 Joseph Sale Shop
*Women's Clothing*

Joseph is something like the J Crew of London—casual clothes and suits for a youngish person of style, but without the rugged outdoorsy element of J Crew. It's become a symbol of sorts; Londoners know their neighborhood is fully gentrified when a Joseph shop opens.

The sale shop on Kings Road is where the company moves marked-down merchandise from the full-price shops elsewhere in town. The selection and range of sizes are limited, but you can find half-price trousers, suits, and tops. Some of these will still seem expensive if you're a bargain shopper.

# ELYSTAN STREET

A BLOCK or so off Kings Road in a little neighborhood called Chelsea Green is Elystan Street, which has several good shops worth visiting.

## 4  Sign of the Times
*Designer Clothing Resale*

ADDRESS
17 Elystan Street
SW3

PHONE
0207 589 4774

HOURS
Mon.–Fri. 10:00 a.m.–6:00 p.m.;
Sat. 10:00 a.m.–5:30 p.m.
$–$$

It's not a secret that even clothing resellers themselves sometimes shop at Sign of the Times. The shop, owned by the vivacious Lorraine Fraser, has been there twenty-six years and has regular customers. It's common to see Fraser bustling around the shop, selecting nearly new suits and dresses for a customer of twenty years. The Gap jeans, Armani suits, and fetching hats here are mostly consigned by fashionable Londoners. Like many London consignment shops, the highest-end items still command high prices—£800 for a Dior suit—but that's a snip of the retail price, and there's much priced well below that.

## 5  La Scala
*Clothing Resale for Men, Women, and Children*

ADDRESS
39 Elystan Street
SW3

PHONE
0207 589 2784

HOURS
Mon.–Sat. 10:00 a.m.–5:30 p.m.
$–$$

An upscale resale shop with modest prices on a big selection of clothes in a good range of sizes, including a dedicated rack of larger sizes. Menswear is downstairs, with racks and racks of lightly worn suits, and plenty of well-dressed gents sifting through them. Also downstairs is a selection of children's clothes in excellent condition.

## 6  Cath Kidston
*Fabrics and Home Décor Items*

ADDRESS
12 Cale Street
(at the corner of Elystan)
SW3

PHONE
0207 584 3232

HOURS
Mon.–Sat. 11:00 a.m.–6:00 p.m.

WEBSITE
www.cathkidston.co.uk
$–$$

BRANCH:
NOTTING HILL
(This is the original location.)
8 Clarenden Cross
W11 (Holland Park Tube)

PHONE
0207 221 4000

Cath Kidston offers very pretty, very English fabric, wallpaper, interior décor items, and a bit of furniture in light, bright florals, stripes, and dots. The look is great for boudoir, sunroom, or children's rooms, but versatile enough to blend into other decorating schemes. Nudge around the corners of this little shop for lampshades, pet beds, covered hangers, ironing board covers, aprons, and serving pieces, all in the signature fabrics. Or take home a few meters of plasticized fabric for covering garden or kitchen chairs. There's a small selection of yummy paint colors in tiny cans with names like "Bunny's Ear" and "Campanula." Get a preview on the website.

# KINGS ROAD

## 7  Octopus
*Clever Gifts, Fun Doodads*

ADDRESS
130 Kings Road
SW3

PHONE
0207 589 1111

(*See page 103.*)

## 8   Antiquarius Antiques

*Antique Mall*

ADDRESS
135 Kings Road
SW3

PHONE
0207 351 4154

About one hundred dealers are clustered into this maze of stalls that offer everything from dusty junk to fine objets d'art.

Go by Malcolm Simpson's stand, E1, for eye-popping quantities of ivory. Many are decorative items, such as cane heads. But others are useful things like letter openers, memo blocks, and cups. If something catches your eye, Simpson has the proper papers required to ship ivory out of the country. (Phone: 0207 352 7989)

C. Negrillo Antiques, stands P1, P2, and P3, has a case of charm bracelets in gold and silver. Her gold bracelets include those with hollow charms, and those with 24-karat charms, so there's likely something in your price range. I found a gold bracelet bulging with 22-karat charms for £900. (Phone: 0207 349 0038; e-mail: negrilloc@aol.com)

There are so many luxe wooden boxes in Gerald Mathias's stall (R5–R8) that you could mistake it for an executive's office. Besides antique boxes, Mathias has tea caddies, desk accessories, and desks, all well chosen, lovely, and seemingly in superb condition. (See his website: www.geraldmathias.com.)

Phillipa Antique and Modern Jewelry, stand J4, stocks distinctly fine antique pieces of jewelry, some quite large and elaborate, others quaint and pretty. Even if you aren't buying, it's worth stopping for a look at what the well-to-do were wearing back when. (Phone: 0207 351 0294)

ADDRESS
178A Kings Road
SW3

PHONE
0207 351 1577

HOURS
Mon.–Sat. 10:30 a.m.–6:30 p.m.;
Sun. 12:00 p.m.–6:00 p.m.
$

## 9   Lucy in the Sky
*Accessories*

Lighthearted accessories with a retro look that will especially appeal to teens and twenties. You may find a kitschy straw bag like the one your grandmother brought back from Hawaii in 1966 (£42). Or fun footwear, such as a pair of pointy-toed colorful sandals (£42.50). Chunky and funky jewelry abounds, such as a faux turquoise-and-silver bracelet (£44.99), or a leather-and-rhinestone cuff (£26.95). For men, there are amusing cuff links, like the pair that say "babe" and "magnet."

ADDRESS
182 Kings Road

PHONE
0207 351 6259

HOURS
Mon.–Sat. 10:00 a.m.–7:00 p.m.;
Sun. 12:00 p.m.–6:00 p.m.
$

BRANCHES:

SOHO
25A Old Compton Street
W1D (Tottenham Court Road or
Piccadilly Circus Tube)

PHONE
0207 287 3789

SOHO/REGENT STREET
45 Carnaby Street
W1F (Oxford Circus Tube)

PHONE
0207 734 1458

## 10   Aware Underwear
*Underthings for Men and Women*

Aware Underwear is a dedicated underwear shop that gives equal space to men's undies. Choose from Hugo Boss, Dolce & Gabbana, Zimmerli, and Calvin Klein in styles from strip-club sexy to practical but not dowdy. You'll find Dolce & Gabbana trunks for £21.95; Zimmerli boxers for £35.50. Half the shop is women's underthings, which edge more toward the sporty, cute, and quasi-athletic than the fetishy, rip-them-off-now variety.

## 11 Daisy & Tom

*Children's Toys, Clothing, and More*

With a working carousel and a puppet theater, this children's store really is for children. It's a great break for those shopping Kings Road with the whole family.

On the ground floor are loads of toys, with good dress-up clothes, magic tricks, craft kits, cute height charts, and a dozen styles of doll strollers, from old-style English prams to double jogging strollers. There's a good sale table, too.

For the U.S. shopper, Daisy & Tom is useful for toys based on English children's television characters, which may be a novelty for the kiddies back home. You probably haven't heard of Postman Pat, Noddy, Sooty, Mr. Men, Brum, or the Fimbles, but they're the stuff of English childhood, and there's a whole section of such toys.

Upstairs is children's clothing, with a big selection of name-brand and designer clothes such as Dolce & Gabbana, Flap Happy, and Petit Bateau.

Also upstairs is an elaborate marionette theater, with several showings a day (call for the schedule). The carousel downstairs offers rides Mon.–Sat. at 11:00 a.m., 1:00, 3:00, and 5:00 p.m.; Sun. 1:00 and 3:00 p.m. (but confirm these times by telephone before you build a trip around it).

ADDRESS
181 Kings Road
(near the old Chelsea Town Hall)

PHONE
0207 352 5000

HOURS
Mon.–Wed. and Fri. 9:30 a.m.–6:00 p.m.;
Thurs. and Sat. 10:00 a.m.–7:00 p.m.;
Sun. 11:00 a.m.–5:00 p.m.
$–$$

## 12 Steinberg & Tolkien

*Fine Vintage Clothing*

Designers, film types, and other performers, as well as mere mortals, browse the collection of 1920s costume jewelry, authentic flapper dresses, Schiaparelli and Dior couture, Zandra Rhodes, Ossie Clark, YSL, and scads of old handbags—for costumes, an awards ceremony outfit, or just ideas.

There's more action downstairs, where there are racks and racks of vintage clothes. You'll have a chore digging through it all, but if you love vintage, it will be worth it

ADDRESS
193 Kings Road
SW3

PHONE
0207 376 3660

HOURS
Mon.–Sat. 11:00 a.m.–7:00 p.m.
$$–$$$

and you'll find something fabulous, if pricey. Many of the clothes originated in the States and came to England with owner Tracy Tolkien, who is an American married to Brit Simon Tolkien.

And the name? Yeah, it's *that* Tolkien family, so, as you'd expect, Tracy has written several books, all of them on vintage fashion, handbags, and jewelry.

ADDRESS
233 Kings Road
SW3

PHONE
0207 351 7728

HOURS
Mon.–Fri. 8:30 a.m.–5:00 p.m.;
Sat. 9:00 a.m.–1:00 p.m.

WEBSITE
www.sanderson-uk.com

$–$$

## 13   Sanderson
*Traditional and Modern Fabrics*

If your taste runs to English fabrics and décor, Sanderson is worth stopping in for florals (ancient, modern, and retro), leaf prints, and botanical themes. As well, there are handsome drawing-room tweeds and lush Eastern-inspired fabrics.

The Morris & Co. line of material is based on the work of nineteenth-century designer William Morris. These distinctive floral and leaf prints are still strongly associated with English country houses, and you could hardly find anything more typically English to take home with you.

If you just want a little Sanderson to tuck into your suitcase, they have bed linens, too, in gorgeous floral patterns.

# 14 Designers Guild

*Fabric, Furniture, and Home Décor Items*

Tricia Guild opened her shop in 1970 and has spent the ensuing years building a design empire. The shop offers wallpaper, fabrics, furniture, bed and bath collections, and accessories, all in Guild's signature brilliant colors and bold designs, which break with traditional "English design" and are therefore very popular with style-conscious Brits. The look is distinctive, and once you've seen it, you can spot Designers Guild products from a long way off.

Designers Guild is a lifestyle concept, meaning that you can sleep on it, eat with it, write on it, sit on it, bathe in it, dry off with it—every moment of your day can be Designers Guild–decorated. Accordingly, there's a bit of everything in the shop, including kitchenware, leather accessories, glorious wrapping paper, and office supplies. If you are looking for a gift, you're bound to find it here.

The contrasting colors and assertive designs suggest retro-futuristic furniture, and there is some of this for sale, from low, squared sofas to clear molded-plastic chairs.

It's also a look that works in a child's room. Perhaps what will most appeal to U.S. shoppers is the DG Kids line of wallpaper, fabrics, sheets, and child-size upholstered furniture. The bright colors are cheerful, and the patterns are very sweet.

Wander around a bit, and you'll find that it's not all lime green and turquoise stripes or giant red flowers. The Designers Guild carpets are quite arresting, in bold but simple patterns and colors.

The website has lots of great photos of the products, so you can preview before you go.

ADDRESS
267 and 277 Kings Road
SW3

PHONE
0207 351 5775

HOURS
Fabric and bed linen stores:
Mon.–Sat. 10:00 a.m.–6:00 p.m.;
bed linen store also open Sun.
12:00 p.m.–6:00 p.m.

WEBSITE
www.designersguild.com
$–$$$

ADDRESS
49 Old Church Street
SW3

PHONE
0207 352 3863

HOURS
Mon.–Fri. 10:00 a.m.–5:30 p.m.;
Sat. 10:30 a.m.–5:00 p.m.

$$

## 15　Manolo Blahnik
*Women's Shoes*

If the television comedy *Sex and the City* is to be believed,
a girl is not complete without a pair of these bare,
teetery designer shoes. If you haven't shopped the New
York store, here's your chance to see the shoes and decide
for yourself whether the £250 pumps are for you. Take
Old Church Street off Kings Road and look on your
right for the discreet, vine-covered façade with display
windows and urns in front. The stratospheric prices are
sharply discounted at the July and January sales.

ADDRESS
285 and 289 Kings Road

PHONE
0207 376 7129; 0207 352 3431

HOURS
Mon.–Sat. 10:00 a.m.–6:30 p.m.;
Sun. 1:00 p.m.–6:00 p.m.

$–$$

## 16　Sukie's Shoes
*Women's Shoes*

Sukie's is probably my favorite London shoe store for
style and price. The shoes are designed by proper shoe
designers, mostly Italian, who design for the big fashion
houses. The shoes at Sukie's are what they make on the
side, and you'll recognize the quality and innovation the
minute you walk in the door.

In addition to the mile-high shoes in fashion at the
moment, you'll see comfortable styles, low heels, and
utterly wearable designs as well as multicolored, high-
design conversation pieces and just plain oddballs. Notice
especially the unique heel treatments and trims. These
shoes represent style, not fashion. Many shoes are priced
around £90, much less than designer-branded shoes.

Sukie's is mindful of the men—half the shop is given
over to men's shoes in the same tasteful-to-zany mode.

ADDRESS
304 Kings Road
SW3

PHONE
0207 352 1456

WEBSITE
www.osborneandlittle.com

$–$$

## 17　Osborne & Little
*Traditional and Modern English Fabrics*

Osborne & Little, one of England's biggest and best-
known fabric retailers, should be at the top of your
shopping list if you're interested in décor. Though the
fabric is available through the design trade in the States,

the London store is open to the public, offering a vast range of fabrics covering its three decades in business.

Choose from fabrics suited to stately homes, quaint cottages, or urban apartments. It's my favorite place to hunt for fabrics because the selection is so enormous, and there's always something perfect (though you may have to dig through decades of out-of-fashion fabrics to find it). The showroom is dotted with little alcoves that show the fabrics made up, which is helpful. Besides their own fabrics, O&L commissions lines from the divine Nina Campbell and pretty Liberty Furnishings.

## 18   Couverture
*Pajamas, Linens, Bedroom Accessories*

Owned by Emily Dyson, of the Britain-based Dyson vacuum cleaner empire, this shop specializes in bedroom things, like pretty embroidered cotton pajamas and blankets, pastel leather slippers, sleep socks, baby blankets, and the like. With all the cotton and pastels, the shop is immensely pleasant to look at and browse. (See the interior on the website; click on "shop.") There's a cute assortment of inexpensive dolls, stuffed toys, baby shoes, mittens, teacups and the like that would make good gifts. Prices: candy-striped voile flat sheet, £103; bias-cut voile nightdress, £72; plain men's white cotton pajamas with topstitching, £145; hand-knitted bed socks, £30 adults, £12 children.

ADDRESS
310 Kings Road
SW3

PHONE
0207 795 1200

HOURS
Mon.–Sat. 10:00 a.m.–6:00 p.m.

WEBSITE
www.couverture.co.uk
$–$$

## 19   William Yeoward Crystal
*Reproduction Crystal*

Furniture designer William Yeoward and third-generation crystalmaker Tim Jenkins have collaborated to reproduce and market reproductions of fine old crystal. Yeoward designed the items with inspiration from existing pieces, taking just what he liked in pattern, feet, and stem treatments from as far back as antiquity, but also from Regency, Georgian, and Victorian styles.

ADDRESS
336 Kings Road
SW3

PHONE
0207 351 5454

HOURS
Mon.–Fri. 9:30 a.m.–6:00 p.m.;
Sat. 10:00 a.m.–5:00 p.m.

WEBSITE
www.williamyeowardcrystal.com
$–$$

The collections include mostly handsome pitchers and drinking vessels from lusty to delicate, but compotes and vases also figure in, as do whimsical items such as a castle-shaped honey pot. Many have ancient influences and others look positively contemporary, with neither a flower nor a garland in sight.

If you've been put off by the dowdiness of crystal, you should visit William Yeoward for a fresh look at what is possible. See some of the designs on the website. His work has a fairly good U.S. distribution network, so check prices.

## 20 Graham & Green
*Gifts, Jewelry, Bedroom Accessories, and Decor*

ADDRESS
340 Kings Road
SW3

PHONE
0207 352 1919

HOURS
Mon.–Sat. 10:00 a.m.–6:00 p.m.;
Sun. 12:00 p.m.–6:00 p.m.

WEBSITE
www.grahamandgreen.co.uk
$–$$

BRANCH:
Notting Hill
4, 7, and 10 Elgin Crescent
W11 (Ladbroke Grove Tube)

PHONE
0207 727 4594

Browsing this gift and décor shop is so rewarding because the selection changes constantly, and every corner holds a treasure waiting to be found. Upstairs, find floaty, faintly ethnic clothes, several cases of jewelry, and pretty bedroom accessories, like nightwear, slippers, candles, and scents.

Downstairs is an unusual and appealing selection of décor items, such as a velvet, metal, and glass doorstop (£22.50); a glass lamp base (£55); etched mirrors; an old carved cabinet from South China (£975); pink leather sequined throw pillows (£45); a cotton rose-pattern duvet cover (£115); or black lacquer rice bowls (£7.50). Preview the goodies in the store on the website in their large online catalog.

## CULTURE ALONG THE WAY

IF YOU began shopping at the top of Kings Road, you'll likely need a break. This section of Kings Road has numerous Italian and European grocers and Italian eateries, if you find yourself in need of sustenance.

ADDRESS
344 Kings Road
SW3

## 21 Brora

(*See page 178.*)

## 22 Opium

*Imported Antiques, Furniture, Décor*

ADDRESS
414 Kings Road
SW10

PHONE
0207 795 0700

HOURS
Mon.–Sat. 10:00 a.m.–6:30 p.m.;
Sun. 12:00 p.m.–6:00 p.m.

$–$$

Opium refers to itself as a "den of treasures and artifacts from India, Morocco, and Asia." Owner Tracy Kitching travels to India twice a year for five weeks at a time to collect architectural pieces and furniture and to pick up her specially designed jewelry.

It's a wonderful place to get inspiration for your decorating projects. I found an antique carved shutter (£255) that would be just the thing in the right room, and an antique sandstone mortar for a doorstop. Maybe the nineteenth-century carved Ganesh door lintel (£200) or a masonry figure (£158) would put the right touch in your house.

For just a flavor of India, there are bone doorknobs by the basket (£3–5), antique porcelain doorknobs (£8), and marble lotus-flower plates (£35 each). For an indulgence, seek out an antique phulkari bagh wedding shawl, years in the making by the groom's mother (£295). At £38, a Burmese lacquer tray would make a one-of-a-kind gift.

ADDRESS
430 Kings Road
SW10

PHONE
0207 352 6551

HOURS
Mon.–Sat. 10:00 a.m.–6:00 p.m.
$$–$$$

BRANCH:
44 Conduit Street
W1S (Bond Street Tube)

PHONE
0207 439 1109

The Conduit Street store is the flagship and has more grown-up clothes, including some of Westwood's signature tartan, and more sizes.

# 23 Vivienne Westwood World's End

*Designer Clothing*

Immediately recognizable by the enormous clock outside spinning madly backward, this shop is where the Sex Pistols got their name and image, and where Westwood made her name on bondage-inspired clothing adorned with holes and zips.

She has continually innovated, developing a Pirate collection with "new romantic" frilly sleeves and nineteenth-century cuts, the infamous fur G-string, tartan wedding dresses, and the mock-crocodile lace-up platform shoes, from which supermodel Naomi Campbell famously fell onto the catwalk in 1993.

Westwood is still designing unexpected clothing, whether zany and barely wearable or just unusual. The World's End shop, named after this part of town but strangely apt, features the punkiest of Westwood's designs. Heads will certainly turn when you show up in platform Mary Janes, a one-armed dress styled like a man's dress shirt, and razorblade-and-safety-pin earrings. The new Red Label clothes, a so-called diffusion line, offer more wearable dresses and even twin sets. Not that they're staid.

# WHERE TO EAT

## Gordon Ramsay

Gordon Ramsay is a destination restaurant for serious foodies. You'll need to reserve a table more than a month in advance, probably before you leave the States, to sample the meal-of-a-lifetime cooking of London's best-known chef. There's a three-course lunch (around £35), a three-course dinner (for around £65), and a seven-course dinner (around £85).

ADDRESS
68 Royal Hospital Road
SW3

PHONE
0207 352 4441

HOURS
Lunch 12:00–2:30 p.m.
Dinner 6:45–11:00 p.m.
closed weekends

## Chelsea Kitchen

Chelsea Kitchen has got to have the cheapest food in London, if not the finest cooking. The restaurant, which is something like a coffee shop, has fed a generation of artists and bohemians, so when you eat there, you're following in the footsteps of London cultural history. The breakfast is dependably good and laughably cheap: 60P for a scone, 90P for a poached egg, £2.40 for an omelet. There's also a daily three-course set menu for about £7 to £8, spaghetti (£3), liver and onions (£3.30), various pasta dishes, fried gammon (that's ham, to you and me), minute steak, and a long list of sandwiches and desserts.

It's not all just grub; there are unlikely upmarket selections such as trout meunière, chicken parmigiana, escalope napolitana, grilled salmon (£4.40), and the traditional final British course of cheese and biscuits. The Chelsea Kitchen also serves wine and beer.

There are nearly always patrons smoking directly underneath the No Smoking sign, so you might wish to request a smoke-free seating area, if possible. It's a good place to people-watch, especially if you get a window table.

ADDRESS
98 Kings Road
SW3

PHONE
0207 589 1330

HOURS
Mon.–Sat. 8:00 a.m.–11:30 p.m.
Sun. 9:00–11:30 p.m.

ADDRESS
350 Kings Road
SW3
PHONE
0207 559 1000
Hours
Lunch 12:30–3:30 p.m., Mon.–Fri.
Dinner 6:00–11:30 p.m., Mon.–Sat.
  6:00–10:30 p.m., Sun.
Brunch 12:00–4:00 p.m., Sat.–Sun.

# Bluebird

Another of the popular restaurants owned by the Conrans, founders of Conran Shops, Habitat, and Heal's. Bluebird is part of a complex that includes a bar and café downstairs, a Sainsbury's supermarket, and a Conran 2 shop.

The restaurant is a vast converted garage that seats about 250 and overlooks Kings Road. The menu concentrates on seasonal produce from small British producers, and fish and seafood in pairings that expertly balance flavors and textures. The offerings change, but expect a typical starter of quail, along with celeriac and hazelnut salad (£8.50), lobster and dill ravioli (£9.75), and extensive oyster offerings (£7.85 to £15.25 for six). Main courses typically include half a dozen fish from £15.75, lamb kidneys, beef filet, Gressingham duck (£17.25), and roast rabbit, all garnished with carefully chosen, well-cooked accompaniments. The wine list is long and thoughtful, with a good selection of both whites and reds by the glass.

Families with children are common here in the early evening. The upstairs bar is very busy and buzzy after 8:00 p.m.

It's quite expensive, though, by American standards. A single fish entrée and a single glass of wine came to £28, or nearly $45. Two courses with wine would average around £35 per person. Lunch and dinner prix fixe menus are not prominently posted and are easier on the wallet at £20 for a three-course lunch. You need to reserve to obtain the prix fixe price.

# CULTURE ALONG THE WAY

## Chelsea Physick Garden

Originally begun as a four-acre collection of medicinal plants and herbs for study, the garden is still used primarily for educational and horticultural purposes, but it is open to the public two days a week. About five thousand plant types are grown in systematic and themed beds: the Dermatology bed, the Aromatherapy Border, Garden of World Medicine, South American bed and such. Entrance fee: £5 adults; £3 students and children.

ADDRESS
66 Royal Hospital Road (entrance on Swan Walk)
SW3 (The 239 bus stops outside the garden.)
HOURS
Open early Apr. to late Oct. (call for precise dates):
Wed. 12:00 p.m.–5:00 p.m.;
Sun. 2:00 p.m.–6:00 p.m.

## Chelsea Pensioners

It's worth visiting the Safeway at 25–27 Kings Road in the mornings to see the retired military officers shopping, nattily attired in their navy or scarlet uniforms. They come from the Royal Hospital around the corner, which is now a retirement complex for army veterans, known as Chelsea Pensioners. (The playing fields of the Royal Hospital are the site of the Chelsea Flower Show in May of each year.) For a pleasant detour from Kings Road, visit the Ranelagh Gardens adjacent to the hospital, which are open to the public but mostly used by the pensioners.

## Cheyne Walk

Strolling along Kings Road, take a left at Flood Street, Oakley Street, Old Church Street, or Beaufort Street and follow the road down to where it nearly runs into the Thames. It's a nice eight-minute walk that takes you to a pretty street called Cheyne Walk. Three Cheyne Walk is the one-time residence of Rolling Stone Keith Richard, while Mick Jagger lived at 48 Cheyne Walk. (Cheyne Walk is in three pieces, so take *London A to Z*.)

# OXFAM CHARITY SHOPS

How does Oxfam do it? This enormous worldwide charitable organization is especially strong in Britain, where it operates well-organized secondhand shops that are good bargain-hunting territory.

They do it by volume and intelligent merchandising. Enter an Oxfam and you'll think you're in a consignment store. There's a book department, a clothing department arranged by color with sizes clearly marked, a section of foreign-produced "fair trade" products (see below), organized bric-a-brac, appliances, a jewelry rack, and a children's section. Some Oxfam shops even have bridal and music departments (such as the one Marylebone, see page 180).

Since Oxfam is Britain's major recipient of secondhand clothing, you are likely to find excellent-quality, sometimes designer, clothes at unbelievably low prices. Expect women's suits for £24, blouses for £10 to £15, and jeans for about the same price.

The Oxfam at 123A Kings Road is an Oxfam Original, a new concept designed to bring in younger shoppers for funky, designer, trendy, and retro clothes. Fashion experts hand-select these items from the mountains of donated clothing.

In 2002, Oxfam sold 27 million items and raised £11 million for its work in alleviating poverty and suffering worldwide.

## FANTASTIC FAIRLY TRADED FOODS

Oxfam shops across London also sell "fairly traded" food products, including honey, coffee, tea, chocolate, coconut, nuts, rice, cereals, snack bars and other snacks. Fairly traded products are bought directly from producers or small cooperatives in developing nations, so the money goes to the producer, rather than to large multinational corporations.

The products are typically very high quality and often organic. The coffees, teas, and chocolate are particularly good, and priced only slightly higher than commercial products.

Oxfam also carries fairly traded home décor items, such as pillows and comforters. The designs are stylishly ethnic, with an emphasis on Indian and African influence, and the workmanship is impeccable. Many Oxfam stores also carry good-quality stationery, greeting cards, children's gifts, and wrapping supplies made by individual producers or cooperatives in developing nations. The quality and design standards of these products are typically high, and the prices are fair.

# BLOOMSBURY AND HOLBORN

$\mathcal{F}$OR HUNDREDS OF YEARS, this part of London has had an intellectual air imparted to it from the sprawling University of London and the British Museum. Where there are learning institutions, there are bookstores: The area bounded roughly by the British Library near St. Pancras station on one side and the British Museum on the other includes London's densest concentration of bookstores.

And where there are antiquities and collections, there will be stamp, coin, and antiquities and collectibles dealers. Some of these appeal as much to the casual shopper as the enthusiast, and you may be surprised at what catches your fancy.

## WHERE TO STAY

There are so many hotels in the Russell Square/British Museum area that you're sure to find one offering what you need at a price that's comfortable for you. At **Myhotel Bloomsbury** (Bayley Street) you can see how the vision of the individual owner's taste plays out in the rooms designed according to feng shui principles. If you prefer a big-name international chain, there's the pricey **Radisson Marlborough** (Bloomsbury Street). You can sample luxurious four-star accommodations and service at the **Montague on the Gardens** (Montague Street), owned by Red Carnation Hotels, which also owns the **Milestone** (*page 109*). There are plenty of clean, spacious, friendly, and affordable B&Bs in the area, too, such as the **Gresham Hotel** (Bloomsbury Street).

### Russell Square Hotel

The Russell Square is easy to spot by its grand Victorian façade and central location just across from the Tube stop overlooking Russell Square. It's a few minutes' walk

ADDRESS
Russell Square
WCI (Russell Square Tube)
PHONE
0207 837 6470

to the British Museum and ten minutes' walk (or a Tube stop) to Covent Garden. The hotel is part of Le Meridien group.

The hotel has a grand, dramatic lobby. Its 380 bedrooms offer mostly traditional English décor, and amenities such as a message service and movie channels are standard. Or choose an "Art & Tech" room, decorated in a high-tech, contemporary style, which is a nice change from the country-house flounciness of London's hotels. The Art & Tech rooms feature plasma screens and powerful showers. There are two restaurants and a bar in the hotel, and thirteen conference and banqueting rooms.

Rates: standard single rooms, £190; doubles, £205. The "ambassador" rooms and "Art & Tech" rooms are slightly more, but all are under £300.

## Blooms Hotel

ADDRESS
7 Montague Street
WC1 (Russell Square or Holborn Tube)

PHONE
0207 323 1717

This little hotel is ideally situated around the corner from the British Museum, and just two Tube stops (or easy walking distance) from Covent Garden. The building's façade is classic eighteenth-century townhouse, and its interior has a pleasant brass-and-leather men's club feel. The twenty-seven rooms are decorated with antiques and old paintings in late nineteenth-century style. There are four "themed" rooms: Pickwick, Theatre Royal, Lords, and Dickens. The bathrooms are fully contemporary.

Blooms has a dining room, a bar with thirty-five single-malt whiskies, and a clubby sitting room with a fireplace and an honor-system bar. The garden out back is a nice spot to enjoy snacks, coffee, and tea in fine

If your luggage is lost, or you're caught by a sudden cold spell or heat wave, CLOTHING DISCOUNT COMPANY, 6 Southampton Row, WC1 (phone: 0207 430 086), is worth a visit for cheap men's name-brand clothes. You'll find Scottish wool sweaters for £10; padded flannel barn jackets for £9.99; wool scarves for £6.99; wool or corduroy jackets for £79.99. The store is very near the Holborn Tube stop.

weather. You're also just around the corner from pretty Russell Square. The retail room rate is £155 for a single; £195 for a double; £220 for one of the themed rooms or a master suite. They are quite willing to discount the price, if you ask.

## Country Inn & Suites

ADDRESS
110 Great Russell Street
WC1 (Tottenham Court Road Tube)

PHONE
0207 637 7777

It's the price and location that make this hotel attractive: £99 for a single; £129 for a double.

The Georgian exterior of the Russell Street Country Inn looks like a London hotel—no giant parking lot, no guitar-shaped swimming pool. The inside is a discount-store version of English country décor that's in good shape and mostly unobtrusive. The rooms are no smaller than most London rooms, with basic amenities: toiletries, ironing board and iron, coffee- and tea-making appliances, modern bath facilities. There's a restaurant in the hotel, and breakfast is complimentary. It's all perfectly adequate, if not luxurious or especially memorable.

Note that there are no family-size rooms.

## St. Margaret's Hotel

ADDRESS
26 Bedford Place
WC1 (Russell Square Tube)

PHONE
0207 636 4277 or 0207 580 2352

St. Margaret's is the kind of B&B hotel that's common all over Europe: high ceilings, light and bright ambiance, homey lounges, and a choice of rooms with their own bath and toilet (£90) or with facilities down the hall (£52.50 for a single). The most expensive room in the place has its own facilities plus a sunroom for £99.50. Even if the décor is a little worn and faded, St. Margaret's offers good basic accommodations in a cheerful, busy, safe, clean, comfortable, and very well-situated place. Confusingly, the sign for the hotel is not near the door, so read the numbers on the house fronts carefully.

# Bloomsbury and Holborn Shopping Area

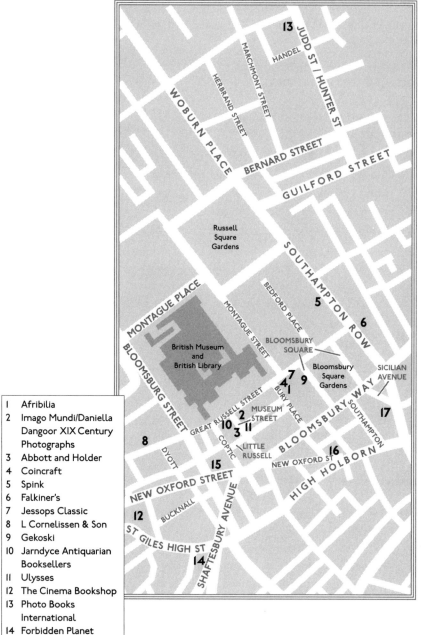

1  Afribilia
2  Imago Mundi/Daniella
   Dangoor XIX Century
   Photographs
3  Abbott and Holder
4  Coincraft
5  Spink
6  Falkiner's
7  Jessops Classic
8  L Cornelissen & Son
9  Gekoski
10 Jarndyce Antiquarian
   Booksellers
11 Ulysses
12 The Cinema Bookshop
13 Photo Books
   International
14 Forbidden Planet
15 James Smith and Sons
16 ModelZone
17 Connock & Lockie

# BLOOMSBURY SHOPS

WITHIN A few square blocks are many shops catering to collectors and to enthusiasts inspired by the cultural and historic riches of the British Museum and abundant in gift ideas and memorable souvenirs.

## 1 Afribilia

*African Collectibles, Antiques, Ephemera*

On a little street across from the British Museum is this shop specializing in African cultural items, antiques, and ephemera. Owner David Saffery grew up in the antiques trade—he learned it from an uncle in South Africa. Saffery travels twice a year to Africa to collect fine and handmade objects such as a palm wine cup from the Kuba people of the Democratic Republic of Congo (£95) and a carved wooden door from eastern Niger (£395). His stock includes furniture, weapons, domestic items, textiles, badges and medals, plus ceremonial items such as figures and staffs and items from the early tourist trade, including an antique beaded Masai flywhisk (£125). He carries some ephemera, including slavery documents from Mauritius and Cape of Good Hope (from £3,900).

There's also a table of inexpensive items such as tin toys made from recycled tin cans in Madagascar, £4.

Saffery reckons he is Europe's only specialist in Rhodesiana, items from Zimbabwe's colonial days, including brass badges worn by native chiefs (from £50). Many of Saffery's items have great stories behind them. You can view some of the collection and read some of the stories on the website.

ADDRESS
16 Bury Place
WCI (Russell Square Tube)

PHONE
0207 404 7137

HOURS
Tues.–Sat. 10:30 a.m.–5:30 p.m.

WEBSITE
www.afribilia.com
$–$$$

ADDRESS
40A Museum Street
**WCI** (Russell Square Tube)

PHONE
Imago Mundi 0207 405 7477;
Daniella Dangoor 0207 404 3919
$$–$$$

## 2 Imago Mundi/Daniella Dangoor XIX Century Photographs

*Maps, Antique Photographs*

If you're a map enthusiast, you'll like the collected items at Imago Mundi, a specialist map store concentrating on antique maps, views, and topographical prints of the world. It's a good choice for hunting up a fine specialty gift. Imago Mundi shares a space with Daniella Dangoor XIX Century Photographs, which offers a small collection of evocative nineteenth-century photographs on paper, albumen prints, photogravures, and salt prints that capture long-ago landscapes and, frequently, faraway subjects.

ADDRESS
30 Museum Street
WCI (Russell Square Tube)

PHONE
0207 637 3981

HOURS
Mon.–Sat. 9:30 a.m.–6:00 p.m.
(open Thurs. until 7:00 p.m.)
$$–$$$

## 3 Abbott and Holder

Abbott and Holder offers three floors of mostly English watercolors and drawings from the fifteenth to nineteenth centuries. The top floor of the shop is designated for conservation and restoration, while the basement holds its framing operation. On Saturdays, the shop gives parents a break by offerings crayons, paper, and plenty of elbowroom to children while parents browse. There's something here for every art budget. I found a watercolor for £1,200, a landscape etching for £675, and a small ink on vellum from a German choir book, authenticated circa 1400, £75.

## 4   Coincraft

*Coins, Antiquities*

Walk out of the British Museum and you'll be headed for Coincraft, where you can buy a bit of the history you've just seen. The family-owned shop deals in coins, banknotes, medals, tokens, and antiquities, but it's the antiquities that are especially interesting to me. Imagine owning a Roman brooch for £125, a Byzantine reliquary cross for £295, a fourteenth-century English crossbow for £35, or a Ming Dynasty terracotta figure for £185. Coincraft has a vast stash of such items, so it's a brilliant place to shop if you want to own a bit of the ancient world.

Pick up their monthly newspaper, the *Phoenix,* which lists their vast holdings, or visit the website.

ADDRESS
44 and 45 Great Russell Street
WC1B (Russell Square Tube)

PHONE
0207 636 1188

HOURS
Mon.–Fri. 9:45 a.m.–5:00 p.m.;
Sat. 9:45 a.m.–3:00 p.m.

WEBSITE
www.coincraft.com
$–$$$

## 5   Spink

*Stamps, Coins, Medals*

Spink is a long-established (1666), highly respected firm that deals in all things numismatic—rare coins, banknotes, medals, and the like. Until recently, it was owned by and integrated with Christie's auction house. Spink publishes and stocks numismatic books, and its *Numismatic Circular* is probably the oldest such publication in the world. The firm holds frequent public auctions on the premises; check the website for dates.

ADDRESS
69 Southampton Row
WC1B (Holborn Tube)

PHONE
0207 563 4000

HOURS
Mon.–Fri. 9:30 a.m.–5:30 p.m.

WEBSITE
www.spink.com
$–$$$

## 6   Falkiner's

*Fine Papers, Bookmaking and Art Supplies*

The full name of this shop is Falkiner's Fine Papers. Artists and book fabricators will swoon over the thirty-three sample books of handmade, textured, and other writing papers. There are also pens and nibs, arcane ink supplies (oxgall solution, carragheen moss, powdered pigments), and leather for hand-making book covers. For the nonartist, there are origami supplies.

ADDRESS
76 Southampton Row
WC1B (Russell Square Tube)

PHONE
0207 831 1151

HOURS
Mon.–Sat. 9:30 a.m.–5:30 p.m.
(closed 1:00 p.m.–2:00 p.m. Sat.)
$

ADDRESS
67 Great Russell Street (entrance in
rear, through Pied Bull Yard)
WC1 (Russell Street Tube)

PHONE
0207 831 3640

HOURS
Mon.–Sat. 9:00 a.m.–5:30 p.m.

WEBSITE
www.jessops.com/classic
$$–$$$

## 7  Jessops Classic
*Collectible Cameras*

Jessops Classic is a branch of one of the main UK camera shop chains, offering classic and collectible cameras. They have a big selection, but they specialize in Leica, Nikon, Canon, Pentax, Zeiss, and Russian-brand cameras. See their online catalog.

ADDRESS
150 Great Russell Street
WC1 (Russell Square or Tottenham
Court Road Tube)

PHONE
0207 636 1045

HOURS
Mon.–Fri. 9:30 a.m.–5:30 p.m.;
Sat. 9:30 a.m.– 5:00 p.m.

$

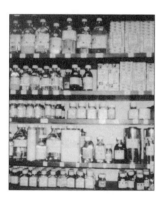

## 8  L Cornelissen & Son
*Fine Art Supplies*

Cornelissen is known outside the art world primarily for its fetching interior—it was, and still looks like, a nineteenth-century Victorian apothecary, with hundreds of wooden drawers and shelves. The space itself is a pleasure to view, especially if you're an artist.

Calligraphers and illustrators go for the vast selection of nibs, pens, and specialty inks. Gilders are drawn to the gold and silver leaf and burnishing supplies. But the store's real pride is its pigments—for printmakers, restorers, painters, and decorators.

Cornelissen was dubbed one of Europe's fifty finest shops in *Trading Places: Europe's Finest Specialty Shops.* If you plan to shop here, look for one of the coupons (called gift vouchers) Cornelissen periodically runs in art magazines (try the calligrapher's magazine called *The Edge*).

# BLOOMSBURY BOOKSHOPS

FOR A complete list of the many antiquarian and secondhand book dealers in the Bloomsbury area, including proprietors' names and telephone numbers, visit www.jarndyce.co.uk.

## 9  Gekoski

Gekoski specializes in twentieth-century literary manuscripts, first editions, and literary painters and illustrators. I once spotted a first edition of T. S. Eliot's *The Waste Land* here for a cool £40,000, but other highly desirable titles can be had for less. Among other delights, the latest catalog lists several first-edition Hemingway books and a copy of John Crowe Ransom's *Grace After Meat*, hand-printed and published by Leonard and Virginia Woolf.

ADDRESS
Pied Bull Yard
15A Bloomsbury Square
WC1A

PHONE
0207 404 6676

## 10  Jarndyce Antiquarian Booksellers

Jarndyce has a large inventory from every imaginable genre, including fine rare eighteenth- and nineteenth-century poetry, art, archaeology, history, literature, and oddities. The travel collections are exceptional, featuring many volumes from the period of great British exploration.

Jarndyce publishes several expert, highly readable catalogs each year that are a pleasure to peruse. The website is also very good.

ADDRESS
46 Great Russell Street

PHONE
0207 631 4220

HOURS
Mon.–Fri. 10:30 a.m.–5:30 p.m.

WEBSITE
www.jarndyce.co.uk

ADDRESS
40 Museum Street
WCI (Holborn or Russell Square
Tube)

PHONE
0207 831 1600

## 11   Ulysses

Ulysses is crammed floor to ceiling with a large stock of twentieth-century first editions (mostly first UK editions) and offers an affordable way to own something special by a favorite writer. Browsing the shelves may turn up an Ezra Pound volume with a review slip for £125, a signed copy of an E. M. Forster work for £75, or a Sylvia Plath limited edition for £45. The nicest, best-pedigreed books are upstairs. Downstairs, less-famous authors or less-favored titles in rougher condition make for happy bargain hunting. Ulysses publishes four catalogs a year.

ADDRESS
13–14 Great Russell Street
WCI (Holborn or Russell Square
Tube)

PHONE
0207 637 0206

## 12   The Cinema Bookshop

Indulge an interest in pop culture with a browse through this bookshop's large selection of books and materials related to film. Besides new, rare, and out-of-print books on cinema, it offers scripts, posters, brochures, stills, and film ephemera.

ADDRESS
99 Judd Street
WCI (Holborn or Russell Square
Tube)

PHONE
0207 813 7363

HOURS
Wed.–Sat. 11:00 a.m.–6:00 p.m.

WEBSITE
www.pbi-books.com

## 13   Photo Books International

This shop offers new and secondhand photography books. Search the website before you go.

# HOLBORN SHOPS

## 14  Forbidden Planet

*Action Figures, Comics, Graphic Novels*

Action figure collectors and fans of graphic novels flock to Forbidden Planet for the biggest selection and latest releases. Shelves are stacked high with action figures, from the Simpsons to Matrix, Hulk to Tony Hawk, X-Men to Transformers. The back room is always crowded with people browsing the shelves and shelves of graphic novels. The shop moved in September 2003 from its former location on New Oxford Street around the corner to Shaftesbury Avenue.

ADDRESS
179 Shaftesbury Avenue
WC2 (Tottenham Court Road Tube)

PHONE
0207 420 3666

HOURS
Mon.–Sat. 10:00 a.m.–7:00 p.m.;
Sun 12:00 p.m.–6:00 p.m.
$

## 15  James Smith and Sons

*Walking Sticks, Umbrellas*

Established in 1830, James Smith and Sons is the last of the custom walking-stick makers in London. If you "go with a stick," the English term for using a cane, they have many handsome examples around £35. Or if you just need a good umbrella, they have those, too, from cheapies for a sudden downpour to £90 models with style and heft. Knobby hiking sticks run about £25. They also have a custom-design service for ceremonial sticks. Get a look at the inside of this charming shop on the website.

ADDRESS
53 New Oxford Street
WC1, Holborn (Tottenham Court Road Tube)

PHONE
0207 836 4731

HOURS
Mon.–Fri. 9:30 a.m.–5:25 p.m.;
Sat. 10:00 a.m.–5:25 p.m.

WEBSITE
www.james-smith.co.uk
$–$$

ADDRESS
202 High Holborn Street
WCI (Holborn Tube)

PHONE
0207 405 6285

HOURS
Mon.–Sat. 9:30 a.m.–6:00 p.m.
$

## 16  ModelZone
*Transportation Models*

For people who love things that go, this big store is the stuff of dreams. Model planes, cars, trucks, rockets, tanks, and trains from die-cast metal to plastic. Some collectible miniatures and remote-controlled toys, too. There are plastic model kits for as little as £9.99 for a North Sea fishing trawler; miniature metal fire engine, £65; World War II Messerschmitt model kit, £24.99; miniature London 1938 tube carriage, £27.99. Need some fake deadfall or simulated woodland flowers for your train set? They have them, along with various paint formulas and other accessories.

ADDRESS
6 Sicilian Avenue

PHONE
0207 636 7260
$$$

## 17  Connock & Lockie
*Custom Tailor*

Occupying a shop in handsome, colonnaded Sicilian Place, this father-and-son bespoke tailor has all the distinguished clients and expertise of Savile Row, but a lower profile and none of the intimidation.

Co-owner Tim Craig displays account books dating back one hundred years to the beginnings of the shop. Downstairs hang suit patterns forty years old, waiting for the customers—or their grandchildren—to return for another suit. It does happen, which is why father and son William and Tim Craig keep the patterns for so long.

The Craigs' suits cost about £1,100; their cashmere coats about £2,000. The process typically includes three fittings over several weeks, or, as in the case of some of Craig's foreign clients, whenever you're in town. Once the pattern is made, your suits can be completed with just an additional fitting or two. The otherwise traditional suits have a bit of fun—the Craigs line their jackets and coats with flamboyantly brilliant silks.

# WHERE TO EAT

## Abeno

This simple, spare, and attractive Japanese restaurant serves okonomi-yaki, a sort of omelet-pancake cooked on your table's sunken grill. Your server mixes up eggs, vegetables, garlic, and ginger and cooks it right there, then decorates it with mysterious but delicious sauces, sprinkles, and shavings. It's cheap (about £7), fresh, tasty, and informal.

ADDRESS
47 Museum Street
(right outside the British Museum)
WCI

PHONE
0207 405 3211

HOURS
Open for lunch and dinner

WEBSITE
www.abeno.co.uk

## Il Castelletto

This is the kind of small, old-fashioned Italian place you'd find in New York. Run by the same family, the Bragoli brothers, for forty years, Il Castelletto is settled and unpretentious, with a menu, and prices, that might have been in place at its grand opening. Starters of mussel soup, prosciutto and melon, and pasta fagioli soup all are under £6. Pastas such as arrabbiatta hover around £5.95, while main courses such as osso buco go for £9.95. Most of the wines are around £14 a bottle. The food is good, if not innovative, and the pink-clothed tables are mostly full of regulars. You don't need a reservation for lunch, usually, but they're a good idea at dinner.

ADDRESS
17 Bury Place
WCI

PHONE
0207 405 2232

HOURS
Lunch from 12:00 p.m.
Dinner from 6:00 p.m.

ADDRESS
43 New Oxford Street

PHONE
0207 836 1011

HOURS
Mon.–Sat. 12:00 p.m.–11:00 p.m.,
Sun. 12:00 p.m.–10:30 p.m.

WEBSITE
www.italiankitchen.uk.com

## Italian Kitchen

For a more contemporary Italian meal, try the Italian Kitchen, which offers a full complement of pizzas and pastas in an informal setting at low prices. Pastas such as tortellini with spinach and ricotta or tagliatelle with salmon are priced between £5.95 and £6.95. Main courses such as roast lamb and baby vegetables, roast cod with chorizo and butter beans, or roast sea bass with couscous are a great value at £9.95. A two-course set menu is £7.95 at lunch. Wines are inexpensive, especially if you catch one of the promotions. One week, two large pizzas and a bottle of wine cost £14.50. The website is very helpful; you can view the menu, get a map, and make reservations, all online.

ADDRESS
4A Streatham Street
WC1 (Tottenham Court Road Tube)

PHONE
0207 323 9223

## Wagamama

(*See page 124.*)

# CULTURE ALONG THE WAY

## British Museum

Deciding what to see in Britain's premier museum is overwhelming, so take the ninety-minute Highlights tour (about £8, offered three times a day) to get an overview. There's also a Highlights audio tour (£3), available in a family version. This last is ideal for children—you'll be surprised by how long the tour can keep your youngster engaged. Or, if you know what you want to see, take one of the free Eye-opener tours, which concentrate on a specific collection. I recommend the American Indian rooms; there are probably more artifacts here than in most U.S. state museums. Children love the Egyptian rooms, with their extensive collection of mummies.

ADDRESS
Great Russell Street
WC1
Phone
0207 323 8299
Hours
Sat.–Wed. 10:00 a.m.–5:30 p.m.
Thu.–Fri. 10:00 a.m.–8:30 p.m.

## Coram's Fields

After a long day of museum-going, turn kids loose at this secure adventure playground and park. Seven acres of things to climb on, sandpits, swings, slides, fenced playground for toddlers, and an animal enclosure. There's also an activity center with an art program and other amusements. Adults accompanying children only.

ADDRESS
93 Guildford Street
WC1 (Russell Square Tube)
HOURS
9:00 a.m.–dusk daily

## Olde Mitre Tavern

Tucked down a narrow alley between Holborn and the City is the Old Mitre, one of London's oldest, most picturesque pubs. This pub was formerly part of the Bishop of Ely's London palace complex in Hatton Gardens. The palace complex was built in 1300, and the Olde Mitre was constructed on the grounds in 1546 for the servants' use.

Queen Elizabeth I strong-armed the bishop into leasing fourteen acres of the grounds to one of her favorite courtiers, Sir Christopher Hatton. A cherry

ADDRESS
Hatton Gardens
EC1 (Chancery Lane or Farringdon Tube)
PHONE
0207 405 4751
HOURS
Mon.–Fri. 11:00 a.m.–11:00 p.m.; closed weekends.

tree, around which Elizabeth is said to have performed a Maypole dance, marked the boundary between Hatton's property and the bishop's. The trunk of that tree is preserved in a display case in the front bar.

The pub was actually under the jurisdiction of Cambridgeshire until about twenty-five years ago. Cambridgeshire issued its license and the Crown owned the property, so London police had no jurisdiction there. The area around the Olde Mitre, Hatton Gardens, is the gold district, and more than one jewel thief has made a dash for the pub's police-free sanctuary.

Next door, the church of St. Ethelreda was formerly the private chapel of the palace. It's the only building in London to survive from the reign of Edward I (1239–1307). A model of the old palace is on display in the church's crypt.

The pub is tricky to find: It's down a sort of alleyway between 8 and 9 Hatton Gardens. Or, if you're on Charterhouse, turn into Ely Place. Snacks only—no meals served.

# SOHO AND CHARING CROSS

THIS AREA, BORDERED BY wealthy Mayfair on one side and Regent Street on the other, was once London's hunting ground, and takes its name from the ancient hunting cry "Soho!" The area's winding streets are a mixture of retail, clubs, and office space, of media industry workers, bohemians, club types, and sex industry workers, a holdover from Soho's grittier past. The retail here tends toward independently owned specialty shops.

Charing Cross is best known as an area dense with bookstores selling new and second-hand books.

## WHERE TO STAY

### Charlotte Street Hotel

Charlotte Street Hotel, opened in 2000, is one of the new breed of boutique hotels, situated amid the media land of Soho, near the theater district.

There are two comfy drawing rooms situated on the ground floor where you can retire with your knitting or newspaper. The fifty-two guest rooms feature original artwork, thick, fluffy beds, and light, pretty designer décor. Baths are granite and oak. Every communications/electronic gadget you might need is here, too. The hotel has a gym and a private screening room with Italian leather chairs.

ADDRESS
15–17 Charlotte Street

PHONE
0207 806 2000 (For reservations, call 0207 806 2000 or e-mail charlotte@firmdale.com.)

WEBSITE
www.firmdale.com

Oscar, the hotel's restaurant, is situated on the ground floor adjacent to the lobby. The restaurant has an open-plan kitchen and serves modern British food. Doubles from £210 plus tax.

## Soho and Charing Cross Shopping Area

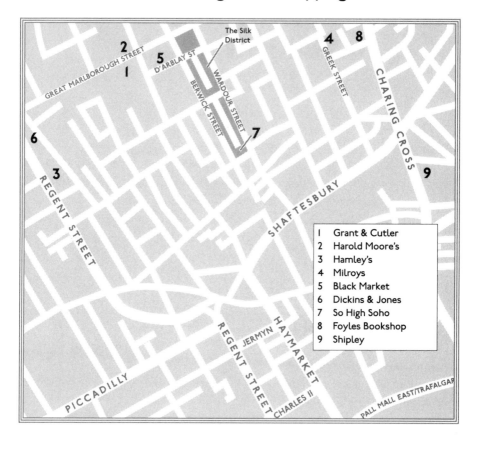

1   Grant & Cutler
2   Harold Moore's
3   Hamley's
4   Milroys
5   Black Market
6   Dickins & Jones
7   So High Soho
8   Foyles Bookshop
9   Shipley

# SHOPPING

## 1 Grant & Cutler

*Foreign Language Bookstore*

This is the UK's largest foreign-language bookstore, and browsing here makes you feel so brainy. Need a Hungarian version of Scrabble? Want to *Teach Yourself Xhosa?* How about Harry Potter books in German? Russian bodice-rippers? Grant & Cutler is a combination of all the things you might want in a foreign-language store. Great for phrase books and travel books, but also for language-learning software, the classics in their original language, a selection of foreign-language novels, critical theory, and films. Non-native speakers will find a selection of British travel guides here, too, in their own languages. There's a small selection of newspapers and periodicals as well. The children's section has excellent choices if you hope to raise a multilingual child.

ADDRESS
55–57 Great Marlborough Street
W1F (Oxford Circus Tube)

PHONE
0207 734 2012

HOURS
Mon.–Fri. 9:00 a.m.–6:00 p.m.
(open Thurs. until 7:00 p.m.);
Sat. 9:00 a.m.–5:30 p.m.;
Sun. 12:00 p.m.–6:00 p.m.

E-MAIL
enquiries@grantandcutler.com
$

## SEX IN THE CITY

Soho has the reputation of having a high concentration of sex shops and strip clubs, and despite a push to license and therefore limit the trade a couple of decades ago, there are still a lot of hookers around, with a particular concentration on and around Brewer Street. The short stretch of Great Windmill Street between Brewer and Shaftesbury Avenue appears to be a twenty-four-hour prostitution zone. At night, the Soho Square Park is a popular rendezvous point for gay men.

ADDRESS
2 Great Marlborough Street
WIF
PHONE
0207 437 1576
WEBSITE
www.hmrecords.co.uk
E-MAIL
sales@hmrecords.demon.co.uk
$

## 2   Harold Moore's

Musically, there's more to Soho than the nightclub beat. Harold Moore's has a reputation among classical music buffs, and when you see the basement, you can understand why. The walls and floor are chock-a-block with secondhand vinyl classical records—boxes and boxes, bins and bins of them. If you like, you can shop and have it shipped to you. If you can't find what you're looking for, register with them, and they will keep a record of the request and let you know if your treasure arrives.

The upstairs, featuring mostly newer releases on CD, isn't too shabby either. If you need early French music or Baltic piano concertos or the soundtrack to *Elizabeth*, it's here. They also maintain a good website, and take e-mail requests for records.

ADDRESS
188–196 Regent Street

## 3   Hamley's
*Toys*

(*See page 99.*)

## 4   Milroys

*Specialty Whiskies*

Milroys is a destination for lovers of Scotch whiskey. The list of Scotch single malts they carry runs to seven pages of small print, ranging in price from £13 for Glenfiddich Reserve to £1,800 for a bottle of forty-year-old Glenfarclas. Milroys has access to some of the rarest vintages around, some as old as seventy-five years.

They will ship purchases, but only if you're prepared to pick them up at the port/airport and pay duty. Better just to tuck a bottle of something rare and fine in your luggage. Better still, try their selection of miniatures—they carry about fifty Scotch and Irish whiskies in miniature bottles. Can't manage that? Then settle for a connoisseur's poster of the Scotch-producing regions of Scotland.

The shop added a cozy bar in the basement in early 2003 to serve its whiskies, and also as a tasting area. Pay £15 and taste whiskies and wines to your heart's content, plus bread and cheese and other goodies. This is a popular spot, so reserve beforehand.

ADDRESS
3 Greek Street
W1V (Tottenham Court Road Tube)

PHONE
0207 437 9311

HOURS
Mon.–Sat. 10:00 a.m.–9:00 p.m.
Bar: 12:00 p.m.–11:00 p.m., but you must enter by 9:00 p.m.
$–$$

### BERWICK'S DAYTIME SCENE

The Berwick Street Market, along the pedestrianized south end of the street, makes for better people-watching than shopping. Among the fruit and vegetable stalls is a scattering of vendors hawking knockoff handbags and CDs.

# SPEED LIMIT: 33⅓ RPM

The DJs who keep up the "two turntables and a microphone" beat of Soho's nightclub scene stock up on the latest house, trance, and techno releases at more than a dozen record stores along Berwick, D'Arblay, Wardour, and surrounding streets. Some of these shops offer CDs as well, but vinyl rules the day at places like **Music and Video Exchange** (95 Berwick Street; phone 0207 434 2939). Here you'll find carton upon carton of twelve-inch discs to suit tastes ranging from "Japanese Techno" and "Nu-Balearic Beats" to "Manchester Indie" and "Future Folk."

**Vinyl Junkies** (in the cellar of 9 Berwick Street; phone 0207 439 2775) specializes in what the guy at the counter calls "proper house music."

**Mad Records,** 2 Silver Place, is located down an alley running south from Broadwick Street. (Phone: 0207 439 0707; website: www.madrecords.net)

ADDRESS
25 D'Arblay Street
W1 (Tottenham Court Road or
Oxford Circus Tube)

PHONE
0207 437 0478

HOURS
Mon.–Sat. 11:00 a.m.–7:00 p.m.

WEBSITE
www.blackmarket.co.uk

$

## 5   Black Market
*House, Drum and Bass, Jungle Music on Vinyl*

Black Market is a must-visit for DJs and fans of dance music and culture, the place to find house music (on vinyl, of course) and drum and bass (in the "drum and bassment," naturally). If you came to London to party and dance, start here; the back room holds racks of fliers promoting upcoming parties, sessions, and club dates. Their website offers loads of Real Audio files, news and updates, webcams, and shopping.

## 6   Dickins & Jones

*Department Store*

(*See page 98.*)

ADDRESS
96 Berwick Street
PHONE
0207 287 1295
$

## 7   So High Soho

The retail climate of this end of Berwick is pretty well epitomized by **So High Soho,** where you can choose from a wide variety of Hacky Sacks and pick up the latest issue of *Weed World* magazine.

ADDRESS
224–244 Regent Street

# CHARING CROSS BOOKSHOPS

## 8   Foyles Bookshop

Foyles has embarked on its second century without the eccentric charms—books arranged by publisher rather than author, for instance—that endeared it to customers ranging from Walt Disney and Marlene Dietrich to Muammar al-Qaddafi and King Tupou of Tonga. But the current generation of family owners has maintained the shop's commitment to stocking an astonishing range of titles, while refurbishing the store and branching out to take over the nearby **Silver Moon Women's Bookshop** and **Ray's Jazz Shop,** which are now housed within Foyles.

ADDRESS
113 Charing Cross Road
WC2 (Tottenham Court Road Tube)
PHONE
0207 437 5660
HOURS
Mon.–Sat. 9:30 a.m.–8:00 p.m.;
Sun. 12:00 p.m.–6:00 p.m.
WEBSITE
www.foyles.co.uk
$

## 9   Shipley

(Formerly Zwemmer's.) Veteran bookseller Ian Shipley purchased the two famed art and photography shops at 70 and 80 Charing Cross Road, as well as the stock from other Zwemmer's shops, from bankruptcy trustees in 2003. So far, Shipley is showing due reverence to the musty atmosphere that has drawn rumpled, tweedy bibliophiles and print hunters to Zwemmer's since its glory days of the 1930s, when the shop put on the first London gallery shows of the work of Picasso and Dali.

ADDRESS
70 Charing Cross Road
WC2H (Tottenham Court Road Tube)
PHONE
0207 836 4872
HOURS
Mon.–Sat. 10:00 a.m.–6:00 p.m.
$

# WHERE TO RELAX AND/OR EAT

## Toucan

ADDRESS
19 Carlisle Street
WID
PHONE
0207 437 4123

Soho is media land, and the Toucan is a hangout for media people and locals looking for a pint of Guinness or a Jameson's. A bit cramped, but there's a big collection of Irish whiskey, between thirty and fifty at any time, some of them very rare.

## Café Mezzo/Mezzonine

ADDRESS
100 Wardour Street
WIF (Leicester Square or
Tottenham Court Road Tube)
PHONE
0207 314 4000 (for both
restaurants)
Hours
Lunch 12:00–3:00 p.m. Wed.–Fri.
Dinner 5:30 p.m.–1:00 a.m.
  Mon.–Wed.;
  5:30 p.m.–3:00 a.m., Thu.–Sat.
Closed on Sunday
$

For those in a Mediterranean mood, Café Mezzo offers star restaurateur Terence Conran's sublime riffs on Lebanese, Turkish, and Greek cuisine, served in an atmosphere of cool jazz and cool people. With starters from around £6, main courses from £14, and a two-course lunch (and pre-theater dinner) from £13.50, Mezzo offers better-than-usual value for money. Reservations recommended.

Upstairs, there's a second restaurant called Mezzonine, which serves big bowls of inexpensive Asian and Thai-influenced food in a bar setting. Here, a two-course lunch and pre-theater meal is under £10. Reservations recommended for large parties or weekend dinner.

## Japanese Cuisine

Japanese food has been much in vogue in Soho for the past few years. Competition makes for good quality, and the numerous sushi bars and noodle joints of Soho tend to meet a fairly high standard of value for money. **Kulu Kulu Sushi** (76 Brewer Street; phone: 0207 734 7316) is one of several *kaiten* (conveyor belt) sushi factories in the neighborhood. Those craving a hearty slurp of yaki udon can find it served up hot and fast at **Satsuma** (56

Wardour Street; phone: 0207 437 8336). Along the quieter northern fringes of Soho, the **Soba Noodle Bar** at 38 Poland Street (phone: 0207 734 6400) serves up competent grub at a reasonable price. The international **Wagamama** chain of vaguely Japanese noodle bars has a Soho outpost at 10A Lexington Street (phone: 0207 292 0990), as does the ubiquitous **Yo! Sushi** (52 Poland Street; phone: 0207 287 0443).

## Bodean's Barbeque

Bodean's is a double rarity in England—a kid-friendly restaurant and a vendor of passable pork and beef delicacies à la Texas, North Carolina, and points in between.

ADDRESS
10 Poland Street
W1F (Oxford Circus Tube)

PHONE
0207 287 7575

HOURS
Mon.–Fri. 12:00–3:00 p.m.,
    6:00–11:00 p.m.
Sat.–Sun. 12:00–11:00 p.m.

## Fino

Fino is technically in Fitzrovia, but it's just a block or two out of your way. This tapas restaurant is the hot spot of the moment in restaurant-mad London. It's the kind of place restaurant reviewers love—stylish, medium price, excellent food. Fino's tapas are perfectly cooked, a pleasure to eat. Seafood is the specialty, so expect great things of the grilled sardines, squid and ink croquetas, and bacalao fritters. Prices range from £3 for potatoes to £12 for foie gras. If you are overwhelmed, choose one of the two set menus, and be sure to order a Spanish white or red from the bountiful wine list.

ADDRESS
33 Charlotte Street
(entrance on Rathbone Street)
W1

PHONE
0207 813 8010

HOURS
Lunch: Mon.–Fri.
12:00 p.m.–2:30 p.m.
Dinner: Mon.–Sat.
6:00 p.m.–10:30 p.m.
Reservations recommended.

ADDRESS
44 Old Compton Street
WID

HOURS
Mon.–Fri. 7:30 a.m.–8:30 p.m.;
Sat. 8:00 a.m.–8:30 p.m.;

# Patisserie Valerie

Patisserie Valerie houses a bakery/confectionery downstairs, and a fifty-seat café upstairs. Soho is the first branch of this burgeoning chain, now with several branches around central London. The marzipan animals recall Paris's candy shops, the pastries ooze cream and jam fillings, and the tarts glisten under their glaze. Valerie's baked goods taste as good as they look and may be the best pastries in London, so if you can't make it for a meal, try coffee and dessert.

Upstairs, the café serves rather good pastas, meat dishes, and an all-day English breakfast that Londoners love. At lunch, the place is heaving with students and media types, and you will have to wait for a table. Food is served in the evening until 8:30, making it an inexpensive option for dinner. Wine, beer, and spirits are available. Several branches of Patisserie Valerie have opened around London, most offering pastries and coffee plus hot lunches and tea. The food is good and prices reasonable.

BRANCHES:

COVENT GARDEN
8 Russell Street
WC2

PHONE
0207 240 0064

HOURS
Sun. 9:00 a.m.–6:30 p.m.
(Breakfast, lunch, tea, and pre-theater dinners)

KENSINGTON
27 Kensington Church Street
W8

PHONE
0207 937 9574
(Breakfast, lunch, and tea)

KNIGHTSBRIDGE
215 Brompton Road
SW3

PHONE
0207 823 9971
(Breakfast, lunch, and tea. Largest branch.)

MARYLEBONE
105 Marylebone High Street
WIU

PHONE
0207 935 6240
(Breakfast, lunch, and tea)

# CULTURE ALONG THE WAY

## National Portrait Gallery

The National Portrait Gallery is an endlessly absorbing collection of simply the finest portraits on earth. Plan to spend awhile here, studying the faces, the fabulous fabric folds, the light and shadow in these works. They're all here, from Holbein to Gainsborough to Mapplethorpe to Lucian Freud to Cecil Beaton. The gallery has an online search function that includes images of twenty-three thousand of its works, so you can plan your viewing schedule. Admission is free.

ADDRESS
St. Martin's Place
WC2

PHONE
0207 306 0055 (Recorded information line: 0207 312 2463)

HOURS
Mon.–Sun. 10:00 a.m.–6:00 p.m.
(open Thurs.–Fri. until 9:00 p.m.)

WEBSITE
www.npg.org.uk

## The Silk District

If you like to fantasize about the things you could make with fine silk, have a stroll along Wardour, Berwick, and the side streets between them. Here you'll find the center of London's silk trade, concentrated just north of the theater district it grew up to serve. The jointly owned Broadwick Silks (9 and 11 Broadwick Street), Berwick Street Cloth Shop (14 Berwick Street), and Silk Society (44 Berwick Street) are among several fabric shops serving both the costume designers of the Soho stage and adventurous couturiers, amateur and professional alike. When you really need a swatch of see-through leopard print or a few yards of electric green feather-boa, or even something a little more staid and elegant, here's your destination. Staffers at these crowded and colorful establishments tend to be aspiring designers themselves, so you just may be waited on by the next Vera Wang. Other area silk shops include Borovick Fabrics (16 Berwick Street), Soho Silks (22 D'Arblay Street), and Greenscourt Fabrics (24 Peter Street).

PHONE

0795 136 9022

(for daily locations)

WEBSITE

www.LondonFashionBus.com

## London Fashion Bus

This double-decker mobile showroom is the brainchild of fashion entrepreneur Barry Laden, whose Laden Showroom in Brick Lane (amid the postindustrial developments of Spitalfields, north of the City) is one of the establishments that have made that area a hipster magnet. Crammed into the upper level of the vehicle are over fourteen hundred pieces created by forty small-scale, up-and-coming designers. The bus haunts London's West End most days, though you might see it as far afield as Greenwich or Kingston Upon Thames. We found it parked on Wardour Street, where a Westminster traffic patrolman was issuing it a ticket for double-parking, despite the driver's protests that the bus had special authorization. Assuming the fashionistas can sort out such regulatory difficulties, the Fashion Bus could become a local institution.

# MARYLEBONE

*I*T'S SAID THAT LONDON is a city made of villages, though most of them have lost their separate identities. Marylebone, though, still feels like a village, with a distinct high street, lots of residential properties, and its own look. The area got its name from a church once located here, Mary-by-the-Bourne. Marylebone High Street and the streets nearby offer choice shopping with a combination of typical high-street shops and some independent merchants with desirable wares.

Marylebone has lots of cafés, pizza places and other casual eateries, plus several good attractions, including the Wallace Collection, Madame Tussaud's, London Planetarium, London Zoo, the splendid Regent's Park, and the Sherlock Holmes Museum.

## WHERE TO STAY

### Hotel la Place

Hotel la Place is a small, friendly hotel with loads of comforts and amenities, including a wine bar, a breakfast room, dinner every night, and a new feature, the hospitality room, where you can change and shower when checking in early or checking out late. There's a tiny Internet room with a library of books left by previous guests. A fax is available in many rooms. All rooms have TV, hair dryer, trouser press, tea- and coffee-making facilities, mini bar—everything you need.

ADDRESS
17 Nottingham Place
W1
PHONE
0207 486 2323

Many of the hotel's guests are American (and the proprietors, Hal Jaffer and his mother, lived in the U.S. for several years), so you'll find American touches—king-size beds, ice machines, big, fluffy bath towels.

With its caring staff and good security, Hotel la Place is highly recommended for women traveling alone.

The hotel is also a very good value: singles begin at £99; doubles from £125; king or twin doubles from £130; and suites £140–160, but you may be able to haggle a bit when the hotel isn't full.

## Marylebone Shopping Area

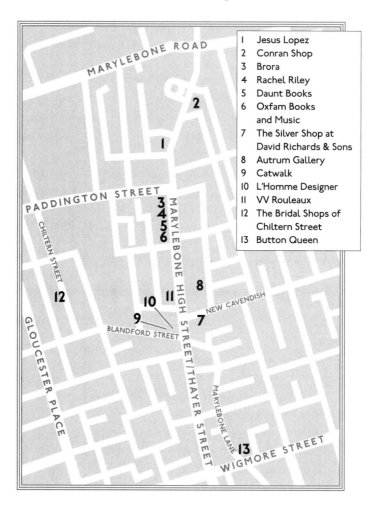

1   Jesus Lopez
2   Conran Shop
3   Brora
4   Rachel Riley
5   Daunt Books
6   Oxfam Books and Music
7   The Silver Shop at David Richards & Sons
8   Autrum Gallery
9   Catwalk
10  L'Homme Designer
11  VV Rouleaux
12  The Bridal Shops of Chiltern Street
13  Button Queen

# SHOPPING

## 1 Jesus Lopez

*Women's Shoes*

Spanish shoe designers such as Lopez are understandably on the ascent in Europe. These individualistic shoes are of all sorts: classic to whimsical, muted to multicolored, and most in styles you'll wear often. Many use a combination of materials, and the majority have decorative details. Prices are good for well-designed shoes, the average hovering around £90. There are a few nice handbags, some pretty clothes, and a case of jewelry.

ADDRESS
69 Marylebone High Street
(Baker Street Tube)
W1U

PHONE
0207 486 7870

HOURS
Mon.–Sat. 10:00 a.m.–6:00 p.m.;
Sun. 12:00 p.m.–6:00 p.m.
$–$$

## 2 Conran Shop

*Furniture, Housewares*

Sir Terence Conran is probably the single biggest influence in how ordinary British furnish their homes nowadays. The Conran Shop is the flagship of a vast empire of home stores, including Habitat and Heal's. For the visitor, it's good for inspiration on indoor and outdoor furniture, bath accessories, and lighting. There's a big kitchen goods department, with shelves and shelves of handsome, modestly priced dishware. The little children's department has a few good toys and cute, well-designed child-size furniture for those tiny British

ADDRESS
55 Marylebone High Street
W1 (Baker Street Tube)

PHONE
0207 723 2223

HOURS
Mon.–Sat. 10:00 a.m.–6:00 p.m.
(open Thurs. until 7:00 p.m.);
Sun. 12:00 p.m.–6:00 p.m.
$–$$$

bedrooms. The Conran Shop is a good bet for hunting up a house-related gift, or a present for the keen cook.

## 3   Brora
*Cashmere*

A wonderful place to find Scottish woollies that you'll love wearing. The cashmere is harvested in Mongolia and processed in Scotland, then made into fashionable, downy-soft sweaters and tops in delicious colors and styles. Besides cardigans (around £180) and pullovers (around £140), you'll find camisoles, v-neck sleeveless T-shirts, and off-the-shoulder styles, plus buttery stoles.

Brora is exceptionally good for baby wear, offering downy-soft baby booties (£19), mittens and hats, blankets (£95), and feather-light little trousers.

Not in the market for clothes? The best value at Brora is the £29 woolen throw rug.

ADDRESS
81 Marylebone High Street
WIU (Baker Street Tube)

PHONE
0207 224 5040

HOURS
Mon.–Sat. 10:00 a.m.–5:00 p.m.
$–$$

BRANCHES:
KINGS ROAD
344 Kings Road
SW3 (Sloane Square Tube, then bus 11, 19, or 22 from Sloane Square)

PHONE
0207 352 3697

NOTTING HILL
66 Ledbury Road
W11 (Notting Hill Gate Tube)

PHONE
0207 229 1515

## 4   Rachel Riley
*Women's, Children's, and Babies' Clothing*

I've always thought it a missed opportunity that Liberty department store doesn't sell clothing made from its signature fabrics.

In fact, when shoppers at Liberty ask for clothing, they're often sent to Rachel Riley. Rachel Riley sells tasteful, handmade clothing for women, children, and babies in lovely, hand-selected fabrics, including Liberty. The emphasis is on ladylike, well-made and elegant clothes. A touch of retro styling adds a timelessness to Rachel Riley frocks, party dresses, print trousers, and blouses. It's not everyone's style, but for handmade clothing, it's some of the best value in London.

ADDRESS
82 Marylebone High Street
WIU (Baker Street Tube)

PHONE
0207 935 7007

HOURS
Mon.–Sat. 10:00 a.m.–6:00 p.m.

WEBSITE
www.rachelriley.com
$$

BRANCH:
KNIGHTSBRIDGE
14 Pont Street
SW1 (Hyde Park Corner Tube)

PHONE
0207 259 5969

It's possible to order Rachel Riley online from the U.S., but the prices are lower in the shop: tops from £79 to around £145; sundresses £140; matching jacket and skirt, £175 and £95; girls' swimsuits, £38 to £45; rose-print pajamas £48; boys' canvas jeans, £42; check shirt, £35; silk gingham party dress, £140. View the collection on the website.

## 5   Daunt Books

*Books*

Daunt Books is usually referred to as a great travel bookstore, but that sells it short. It's an all-around great bookstore in a great space. The nineteenth-century interior is woody but flooded with light from grand stained-glass windows and skylights, and the back room includes a gallery. An abundance of shelf space allows books to be faced out to show the covers. Most Americans are accustomed to this, and it's helpful to customers. It also sells books.

The children's section has a particularly big selection of hardbacks.

ADDRESS
83 Marylebone High Street
W1U (Baker Street Tube)

PHONE
0207 224 2295

HOURS
Mon.–Sat. 9:00 a.m.–7:00 p.m.;
Sun. 11:00 a.m.–6:00 p.m.
$

ADDRESS
91 Marylebone High Street
Phone
0207 487 3570

## 6   Oxfam Books and Music
*Secondhand Books and Records*

This Oxfam shop is notable for its huge and well-organized record section. There are treasures hiding here, and record buffs shop the store frequently. There are also loads of well-chosen books, really cheap, if you're in need of reading material.

ADDRESS
10 New Cavendish Street
WIG (Baker Street or Bond Street
Tube)

PHONE
0207 935 3206

HOURS
Mon.–Thurs. 9:30 a.m.–5:30 p.m.;
Fri. 9:30 a.m.–4:30 p.m.
$–$$$

## 7   The Silver Shop at David Richards & Sons
*Antique and New Silver*

I might not have noticed this little shop off Marylebone High Street where it turns into Thayer Street, except that a Londoner gave me a tip on its low silver prices. This family-run shop has operated for thirty-one years, repairing and valuing silver as well as selling it. Silver photo frames start at £12; silver and semiprecious stone earrings, £55. The little silver tooth-fairy box I picked up was so inexpensive (£28), I thought it was silver plate. But there's also more elaborate merchandise. I spotted a 1912 silver bowl from Birmingham for £600, and a gorgeous silver menorah for £555.

# 8    Autrum Gallery

*Artisanal Jewelry*

Owner and jewelry designer Marion Autrum offers her own designs and those of other selected jewelry artists working in silver, gold, and precious stones. Slip into a necklace of 18-karat hammered gold circles (£1,295), or a monstrous necklace of heavy gold links (£7,000), or a delicate loop of lustrous 24-karat gold. The predominant look here is clean, functional, and almost industrial. If Autrum doesn't stock precisely what you're after, she also takes commissions. See the designs on her website.

ADDRESS
7 New Cavendish Street
W1G (Baker Street or Bond Street Tube)

PHONE
0207 486 8695

HOURS
Tues.–Fri. 10:30 a.m.–6:00 p.m.;
Sat. 10:30 a.m.–5:00 p.m.

WEBSITE
www.autrumgallery.co.uk
$$–$$$$

SLIP ACROSS New Cavendish Street to look at the beautifully designed windows of the **Jane Packer Flower School.** Packer is perhaps best known as the florist who arranged the lilies for the wedding of Sarah Ferguson to Prince Andrew. It's an interior-design sensibility applied to floral arranging, and her windows always offer an inspiration for your own house.

# 9    Catwalk

*Designer Clothing Resale*

Don't be deceived by the size. This small ladies' clothing resale shop is positively bulging with racks of designer duds. Shuffle through the racks, and you'll be rewarded with low prices on Prada, DKNY, MaxMara, and many others. The clearance box is always worth rooting through—the items here are marked down to pennies on the dollar.

ADDRESS
52 Blandford Street
W1 (Baker Street Tube)

PHONE
0207 935 1052

HOURS
Mon. 12:30 p.m.–6:00 p.m.;
Tues.–Fri. 11:15 a.m.–6:00 p.m.;
Sat. 11:15 a.m.–5:00 p.m.
$–$$

ADDRESS
50 Blandford Street
W1 (Baker Street Tube)

PHONE
0207 224 3266

HOURS
Mon.–Wed. and Fri. 11:30
a.m.–5:30 p.m.; Thurs. 1:00
p.m.–8:30 p.m.; Sat. 11:00
a.m.–5:00 p.m.

$–$$

## 10 L'Homme Designer
*Men's Clothing Resale*

Right next to Catwalk is an excellent men's resale shop featuring a good selection of high-quality clothing. Clotheshorses, dandies, and peacocks should definitely put this shop on the list. I found a DKNY long-line tux for £229; a "rock star ready" long, pale purple Versace duster for £229; a Gucci denim jacket for £150. For the smaller ambition, there are the likes of an Ozwald Boateng orange-and-purple-striped tie, an Ermengelda Zegna tie, or a Paul Smith shirt, each £29.

ADDRESS
6 Marylebone High Street
W1 (Baker Street Tube)

PHONE
0207 224 5179

HOURS
Mon.–Sat. 9:30 a.m.–6:00 p.m.

$–$$

## 11 VV Rouleaux
*Ribbons and Trim, Haberdasher*

This branch of the exquisite ribbon-and-trim business is larger than the Sloane Square branch (*see page 66*). Large windows flood the store with light, simplifying detailed color comparisons.

## 12   The Bridal Shops of Chiltern Street

Bridal specialty shops, including menswear, shoes, and made-to-measure items, cluster on Chiltern Street, which intersects Paddington Street at the Marylebone Road end. Here are a few of the bridal stores:

**Melbo** supplies specialty bridal shoes and also makes custom bridal shoes. (Phone: 0207 935 8055)

**By Storm** offers a very big selection of made-to-measure bridal and mother-of-the-bride wear. (Phone: 0207 224 7888)

**Elizabeth Todd** fantasy gowns are based on seventeenth- and eighteenth-century corsetry. Prices start at around £1,400 and go up to £3,500. (Phone: 0207 224 2773)

**Modern Bride** (Phone: 0207 935 3726)

**Gary Anderson**, formal menswear. (Phone: 0207 7224 2241)

**Christine Kendall**, couture wedding gowns and bridal accessories. (Phone: 0207 935 5734)

**Bridal Rogue Gallery**, couture gowns and accessories. (Phone: 0207 224 7414)

**Johanna Hehir**, evening, bridal, and special-occasion wear. (Phone: 0207 486 2760)

## 13   Button Queen

*Antique Buttons*

Button Queen is to buttons what VV Rouleaux is to ribbons. They stock zillions of buttons in little boxes and drawers that can't fail to pique creativity and inspire collectors. Proprietors Isabel and Martyn Frith buy up button boxes and button collections, so they have many vintage and one-of-a-kind sets, and are always looking for interesting buttons if you have them to sell. Get a tiny taste of their selections on the website.

ADDRESS
19 Marylebone Lane
W1 (Bond Street Tube)

PHONE
0207 935 1505

HOURS
Mon.–Fri. 10:00 a.m.–5:00 p.m.
(open Thurs.–Fri. until 6:00 p.m.);
Sat. 10:00 a.m.–4:00 p.m.

WEBSITE
www.thebuttonqueen.co.uk

$

# WHERE TO EAT

Marylebone is unusually dense with good eateries, many of them charming, fair-priced, neighborhood-type places.

**Caffe Caldesi**, tucked away on Marylebone Lane, is very crowded at lunch, so arrive early or telephone for a reservation. Starters such as grilled vegetables with buffalo mozzarella, walnuts, and balsamic hover around £7; pastas around £9; and main courses (fish, lamb, cutlets, chicken) at £14. View the menu at www.caffecaldesi.com.

**Quiet Revolution**, in the Aveda hair/spa salon, is a vegetarian eatery that's said to be good for celeb-spotting.

**Getti**, at 42 Marylebone High Street, gets high marks from locals, but it's pricey—expect £40 for lunch for two.

Paddington Street, which intersects Marylebone High Street, has many good choices. **Zizzi** is an inexpensive pizza place, and **Casa Becci** is always bustling. There's an **All Bar One**, which serves reliably good modern European food at low prices.

Paddington Street also has several French eateries, including **La Galette** and **Du Pain Du Vin**.

ADDRESS
55 Marylebone High Street
W1

PHONE
0207 616 8000

HOURS
Lunch: Mon.–Sun. 12:00 p.m.–3:00 p.m.; dinner: Mon.–Sat. 7:00 p.m.–11:00 p.m.; Sun. 7:00 p.m.–10:30 p.m.

## Orrery

Located on top of the Conran Shop, Orrery is one of many reliable Conran eateries (*see Bluebird, page 144*). The light, elegant Orrery dining room offers fresh, painstakingly sourced ingredients transformed into extraordinary dishes served with quiet professionalism at fairly steep prices.

The menu changes seasonally, but expect starters like terrine of foie gras (£16.50) or lamb terrine; entrées of braised halibut (£25); saddle of rabbit or sweetbreads (£22.50), and risotto with wild garlic and asparagus (£16.50).

If you're not in a hurry, the £23.50 three-course menu du jour is the thing to get. On Sundays, there's a £30 menu, which includes a glass of champagne. It's a leisurely affair—the table next to mine took two and a half hours to get through lunch.

At dinner, the "menu gourmand" offers six courses for £50, or £80 when the courses are matched with wine.

For a less-expensive option, the terrace bar is lovely in nice weather, and has an informal menu of bar food.

Reservations recommended.

## Ard-Ri

The Ard-Ri is the handsome, comfortably old-fashioned dining room above the O'Conor Don, a friendly pub in Marylebone. The well-executed cuisine combines old Irish and new Irish, featuring fresh oysters, beef and Guinness stew, roast lamb, seared tuna with mango salsa, beet-cured salmon, venison with champ (mashed potatoes), and artisanal Irish cheeses.

The wine list is short but well-chosen, with lots of good values. You can reasonably expect a great meal here, with wine, for less than £25.

You can also order from the menu at the street-level bar, even when the dining room is closed between meals.

ADDRESS
88 Marylebone Lane
W1

PHONE
0207 935 9311

WEBSITE
www.oconordon.com

## CULTURE ALONG THE WAY

The Garden of Rest, on Marylebone High Street near the Marylebone Road end, is the site of the old St. Marylebone church. There's been a church in Marylebone since 1400, but this particular church was built here in 1740, closed as a church in 1926, and was badly damaged by the bombing of London during World War II. It was finally torn down in 1949.

The philosopher Francis Bacon was married at the church in 1606. Charles Wesley, brother of Methodism founder John Wesley, is buried in the churchyard. Lord Byron was baptized at St. Mary in 1788, and Lord Nelson was a member of the church. His son Horatio was baptized at St. Mary in 1803.

The sunken part of the Garden of Rest marks the location of the church foundation. The space is open to the public, and is a nice spot for resting after shopping Marylebone.

ADDRESS
Hertford House, Manchester
Square
W1 (Bond Street or Baker Street
Tube)

PHONE
0207 563 9500

HOURS
Mon.–Sat. 10:00 a.m.–5:00 p.m.;
Sun. 12:00 p.m.–5:00 p.m.

WEBSITE
www.wallacecollection.org

# Wallace Collection

Terrific for a one-stop dose of culture and a good meal. The Wallace Collection is housed in what the British refer to as a "stately home." This marvelously refurbished mansion is sumptuously decorated and stuffed with what is said to be the finest private collection of eighteenth-century French pictures, porcelain, and furniture ever assembled. Included in the collection are nearly eight hundred paintings, including works by Bouchard, Watteau, Fragonard, Rubens, Rembrandt, Van Dyck, Canaletto, and Velazquez. Daily guided tours are offered, as is a program of lectures elucidating the treasures. Free admission.

Combine your visit with a meal in the superb restaurant, Café Bagatelle, with its large glass ceiling and salmon pink décor. You will need a reservation in the restaurant.

# NOTTING HILL

The London real estate boom of the 1990s transformed Notting Hill from a neighborhood of longtime residents and West Indian immigrants into a gentrified address for people wishing for a quiet but convenient locale. Quiet, that is, with two exceptions. The Notting Hill Carnival, held in late August, is said to be the largest street festival in Europe, with attendance between five hundred thousand and a million people. And the Portobello Road Market brings in thousands of antique and flea market shoppers each Saturday, as it has for hundreds of years.

With Notting Hill's gentrification have come chain stores and exclusive retail to join the established antique dealers and independently owned shops. Good as the shopping is, it's quite spread out, so make a plan in advance or prepare for a long stroll.

As Notting Hill is largely residential, cultural opportunities are scarce. Still, Notting Hill offers a way for visitors to see where real Londoners live and take in some fine retail.

## WHERE TO STAY

### Pembridge Court Hotel

Pembridge Court Hotel, at the end of Pembridge Gardens, is a tasteful, quietly elegant hotel with all the services you need and none you don't want to pay for. You can guess a little about the clientele when you notice that the hotel has a subscription to *Billboard* magazine. Forty-six rooms, some individually decorated, comprise mostly doubles and a handful of singles. Rooms have TVs,

ADDRESS
34 Pembridge Gardens
W2 (Notting Hill Gate Tube)

PHONE
0207 229 9977

WEBSITE
www.pemct.co.uk

Internet access, air conditioning, and attractively refurbished baths. There are cozy sitting rooms and twenty-four-hour room service. It's in a quiet but well-placed spot near the Notting Hill Gate Tube. Rates: singles from £125; doubles from £160. Family rooms available.

## Hillgate House

ADDRESS
Pembridge Gardens
W2 (Notting Hill Gate Tube)

PHONE
0208 221 3433 (Reservations:
0207 229 6666)

WEBSITE
www.london-town-hotels.com

These five linked townhouses are more impressive outside than inside, and nearby Notting Hill Gate is noisy. Still, all is forgiven when you see the prices. The sixty-four rooms are of average size for London. Amenities are basic but satisfactory, and the hotel has a bar for relaxing and terminals in the lobby for Internet access. Prices vary so much by season and occupancy that they don't publish a rate card, but a standard double in midautumn was £64, while a room for four was £84 a night. Check prices on the website.

## Portobello Hotel

ADDRESS
22 Stanley Gardens
W11 (Holland Park Tube is some
distance away)

PHONE
0207 727 2777

WEBSITE
www.portobello-hotel.co.uk

The Portobello is a boutique hotel so discreetly located that you're upon it before you spot it. A small hotel of twenty-four luxurious, serenely quiet rooms, individually decorated with fine furniture and artifacts, it's supposedly a favorite hideaway of celebrities. While it's off the tourist trail, it's convenient to shopping in Notting Hill and just a few Tube stops from many major attractions. There are business services, access to a health club, interactive cable television, movie channels, and a twenty-four-hour restaurant and bar. Rates: doubles, £160; twins, £180. Have a look at the rooms on the website.

# SECONDHAND MUSIC ON NOTTING HILL GATE

ALONG NOTTING HILL GATE (NHG) are multiple record exchanges: Number 38 NHG sells indie rock, folk, and blues. Number 40 NHG offers vinyl singles, CD singles, and bargain videos. Number 42 NHG sells soul, house, hip-hop, techno, R&B, reggae, funk, and jazz. Number 36 NHG is a classical music exchange. They all buy as well as sell.

# Notting Hill Shopping Area

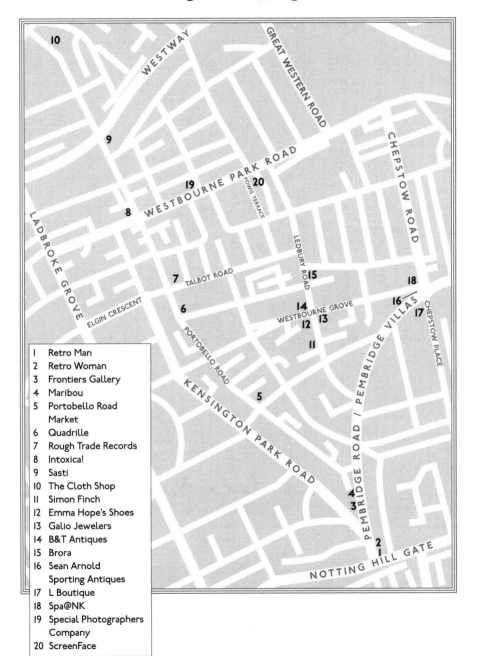

1   Retro Man
2   Retro Woman
3   Frontiers Gallery
4   Maribou
5   Portobello Road
    Market
6   Quadrille
7   Rough Trade Records
8   Intoxica!
9   Sasti
10  The Cloth Shop
11  Simon Finch
12  Emma Hope's Shoes
13  Galio Jewelers
14  B&T Antiques
15  Brora
16  Sean Arnold
    Sporting Antiques
17  L Boutique
18  Spa@NK
19  Special Photographers
    Company
20  ScreenFace

# RETRO SHOPPING ON PEMBRIDGE

THE RETRO shops along Pembridge Road (14–56) are great for one-stop secondhand and vintage shopping. Besides clothing, the Retro empire includes Retro Home (16 Pembridge), Retro book and comic exchange (14 Pembridge), Retro music and video exchange (28 Pembridge), and Retro jewelry and accessories (30 Pembridge). All shops are open 10:00 a.m.–8:00 p.m. every day

ADDRESS
34 Pembridge

PHONE
0207 792 1715

HOURS
Mon.–Sun. 10:00 a.m.–8:00 p.m.
$

## 1 Retro Man

Retro Man is typical of the outstanding secondhand clothing available in London: a YSL jacket for £80; a bespoke suit for £400; Reebok Insta Pump shoes for £40; Miu Miu woven leather shoes for £90.

ADDRESS
32 Pembridge

PHONE
0207 221 2055

HOURS
Mon.–Sun. 10:00 a.m.–8:00 p.m.
$

## 2 Retro Woman

Retro Woman has a big selection of nearly new clothing for the shapely and fashionable: Alexander McQueen bumster jeans, £80; Dolce & Gabbana jeans, £40; Whistles silk capri pants, £25; Miss Sixty boxer-style silk skirt, £40; Agnes B miniskirt, £20; Patrick Cox shoes, £40; Prada wedge shoes, £70; Halston shoes, £70; Miu Miu platform shoes, £70; an undyed pair of Emma Hope's wedding shoes for £80, and Chloe sunglasses for £60.

# NOTTING HILL SHOPPING

ADDRESS
37 Pembridge Road
WII (Notting Hill Gate Tube)

PHONE
0207 727 6132

HOURS
Mon.–Sat. 11:00 a.m.–6:30 p.m.;
Sun. 12:00 p.m.–4:00 p.m.
$–$$

## 3 Frontiers Gallery
*Jewelry, Furniture, Art*

Upstairs you'll find inexpensive ethnic jewelry, totes, pottery, and other affordable and attractive doodads. Downstairs is a selection of reasonably priced mahogany-top tables, Italian-made Lloyd Loom furniture, and garden items. Both are inviting to poke through, and prices are lower than elsewhere in London. There's probably no room in your luggage for a table or some garden furniture, which is too bad, as prices downstairs are very nice.

## 4   Maribou

*Handmade Women's Clothing*

Maribou hand-makes coats, jackets, skirts, and tops, often from old-style fabrics, for a unique look at a modest price. The jackets come in several theatrical cuts—cape, eighteenth-century dandy jacket, smock shapes—in vibrant and dramatic brocades and velvets and billowy cuts that expose the yet more vibrant linings. Skirts are assembled from scarf-like fabrics for a dramatic, fluttery silhouette. There are a few filmy tanks and brocade trousers. You could walk out with a completely new image for a fraction of the cost of made-to-order. Capes around £185; coats around £150; skirts, £85.

ADDRESS
55 Pembridge Road
W11 (Notting Hill Gate Tube)

PHONE
0207 727 1166

HOURS
Mon.–Sat. 10:00 a.m.–6:00 p.m.
(Sometimes open Sun. 12:00–6:00 p.m., but call first.)
$–$$

## 5   Portobello Road Market

The Portobello Road Market is perhaps the Notting Hill destination with the most recognizable name for American travelers. On Saturday, Portobello, Ladbroke Grove, and Golborne roads are lined with stalls and booths. Some fifteen hundred antique dealers alone have stalls, with many more fruit and vegetable stalls, clothing vendors, and flea market booths.

   Antiques prevail toward the Notting Hill Gate end, food toward the middle, while clothes and accessories

HOURS
The general stalls are open all week. Clothing stalls are open on Fri. from about 7:00 a.m.; Sat. from 8:00 a.m.; and Sun. from 9:00 a.m. The antique stalls operate only on Sat., and they open at dawn, so if you're serious about antiquing, arrive by 6:00 a.m.

WEBSITE (ANTIQUES)
www.portobelloonline.com or
www.portobelloroad.co.uk

dominate the end near the Ladbroke Grove Tube stop. Beyond the Ladbroke Grove stop is a flea market, where some treasure lurks among the trash. Professionals are here before dawn with flashlights, looking for things to polish up and resell.

The clothing end is a glorious hodgepodge of stalls and styles, from filmy Indian clothes to knockoffs to vintage to hippy. Look for the designers and importers who sell unique items, often handmade, such as **Comfort Station**'s noveau/retro bags and scarves (see www.comfortstation.co.uk) and the customized English Tea shirts. Also good are the secondhand and vintage stalls, where you'll find great-looking pieces at reasonable prices. There's an unusually deep selection of fur; you can pick up a mink jacket for £95.

The antiques end is also a hodgepodge of furniture, engravings, glass, pewter, antiques, lots of jewelry, clocks—you name it. There are some nice pieces alongside down-at-the-heels pieces and lots of reproductions. See a listing of dealers on the website. Like all antique markets, the dealers here know their merchandise, and their market, well, so dramatic finds and bargains are few. But there's plenty to tempt the average shopper. Londoners shop here joyfully but selectively and with a dose of skepticism. You should, too.

ADDRESS
inside Delehar
146 Portobello Road
W11 (Notting Hill Gate Tube)

PHONE
01923 829 079 weekdays;
0207 727 9860 Sat.

$$–$$$

## 6 Quadrille

*Ephemera*

In forty years of collecting, owner Valerie Jackson-Harris has amassed a fine array of ephemera, a good deal of it from London. It's a pleasure to flip through coronation and other royal commemoratives, tidbits from the performing arts, and "trade cards" from eighteenth-century merchants, any of which would make a fine, if costly, memento of London.

## 7 Rough Trade Records

*CDs and Vinyl Records*

For more than twenty-five years, Rough Trade has been a magnet to those in search of the unusual, obscure, and hard-to-find in music. It was strongly associated with the punk movement and continues to champion the music you won't hear on most commercial radio stations. The place is run by enthusiasts and it shows: For starters, half the stock here is vinyl. In addition, recordings bear stickers that knowledgeably and enthusiastically annotate the contents—it's like shopping with a well-informed friend. Rough Trade occasionally issues its own compilations and sponsors live music, so the shop is as much a community center as a store. It's a good stop if you're looking for live-performance information or just a dose of another culture.

ADDRESS
130 Talbot Road
W11 (Ladbroke Grove Tube)

PHONE
0207 229 8541

HOURS
Mon.-Sat. 10:00 a.m.–6:30 p.m.;
Sun. 1:00 p.m.–5:00 p.m.
$

## 8 Intoxica!

*Secondhand Vinyl Records, CDs*

Intoxica! is a jackpot of used vinyl and collectible records. Sixties soul, R&B, British Invasion, ska, surf, punk—the selection of old vinyl is very good. I found a French release of the Four Tops' *14 Fabulous Favorites* for £18; Ben E. King's *Spanish Harlem* for £7; and the Supremes' Christmas album for £25. The website is comprehensive and frequently updated.

ADDRESS
231 Portobello Road
W11 (Ladbroke Grove Tube)

PHONE
0207 229 8010

HOURS
Mon.–Sat. 10:30 a.m.–6:30 p.m.;
Sun. 12:00 p.m.–5:00 p.m.

WEBSITE
www.intoxica.co.uk
$

## 9 Sasti

*Children's Clothing*

If you started at the Ladbroke Grove end of the market, you'll soon stumble across Portobello Green Arcade. Inside are a number of really interesting atelier shops. Sasti, at number 8, was founded in 1995 by Julie Brown when she was unable to find darling, different, long-lasting children's clothing at affordable prices. The difference starts with the unusual fabrics: tulle, batik,

ADDRESS
8 Portobello Green Arcade
281 Portobello Road

PHONE
0208 960 1125

HOURS
Mon.–Sat. 10:00 a.m.–6:00 p.m.

WEBSITE
www.sasti.co.uk
$

faux fur, puckery plisse, camouflage fleece, panda-print cotton. All the collections are assembled in coordinated groupings by theme, such as western wear, animal prints, punky tartans, fleece and fur. Fleece trousers start at £8, with most trousers, skirts, and jackets in the £20 to £40 range. I loved especially the Vivienne Westwood–style punk tartan trousers (£20) and tops. For a cowboy or cowgirl, western-style fringed jeans (£22) are paired with a fleece-lined vest (£25) and a shirt that says "Yeehaa!" There's a toy corner to keep your young shopper busy while you browse, and a baby-changing area. You can preview the collection on the website.

## TRANSPORTATION MATTERS

Notting Hill's shopping streets are spread over a large area, with nearly a mile between the Ladbroke Grove and Notting Hill Gate Tube stops. Areas east of that, such as Ledbury Road and Westbourne Grove, are not well served by the underground. Look for the number 70 bus, which runs from Ladbroke Grove down Westbourne Park Road and Westbourne Grove (where you can hop off for Ledbury Road) before it winds past Queensway and Bayswater Road stops and comes back to Notting Hill Gate Tube. You'll save some shoe leather and see where ordinary Londoners live.

The number 52 bus is great for sightseeing, as well as useful for traveling from Notting Hill to choice parts of London without the bother of Tube changes. The bus runs several times an hour and stops at Ladbroke Grove across from the Tube station. It travels down Elgin Crescent, then Kensington Park Road, past Notting Hill Gate Tube station, then travels Kensington Church Street (a good place to jump off for Kensington High Street), Kensington Road along Kensington Gardens, Hyde Park Corner, Knightsbridge, and along Grosvenor Place and Buckingham Palace Road to Victoria Station.

## 10   The Cloth Shop

*Selected and Heritage Fabrics*

Owner Sam Harley's grandfather was a tailor, so he knows and loves fabric. He admits, "I have a thing about wool and linen," and it's evident in his loving selections of these fabrics.

He's collected some fascinating wools, cottons, and linens, such as antique Welsh woolen blankets (£70); antique linen sheets (£60 to £90); Indian furnishing fabrics; and heritage British woolens. Devotees of antique fabrics might be interested in an antique mangle cloth, used to wrap clothes before putting them through the wringer (called a mangle in England).

"The thing about this shop is that we really know what we're doing," he says. "I really know about cloth." The U.S. film industry apparently agrees, because it seeks out Harley for its fabrics. He has supplied cloth for the *Pirates of the Caribbean*, the Harry Potter films, *Shakespeare in Love*, and many others.

ADDRESS
290 Portobello Road
W10 (Ladbroke Grove Tube)

PHONE
0208 968 6001

WEBSITE
www.clothshop.co.uk

$

ADDRESS
61A Ledbury Road
W11 (Notting Hill Gate or
Ladbroke Grove Tube)

PHONE
0207 792 3303

HOURS
Mon.–Sat. 10:00 a.m.–6:00 p.m.

WEBSITE
www.simonfinch.com
$$–$$$

## 11 Simon Finch
*Collectible Books*

This shop is a branch of Simon Finch of Maddox Street, in Mayfair (*see page 28*). The Ledbury Road store carries twentieth-century literature, photography and art books, and a bit of design and ephemera. The Finch staff are helpful but laid-back professionals who make book collecting seem contagiously fun and easy, rather than arcane and exclusive. Visit their excellent website to get a feel for their easygoing, accessible style.

ADDRESS
207 Westbourne Grove
W11 (Notting Hill Gate Tube)

## 12 Emma Hope's Shoes

(*See page 64.*)

ADDRESS
201 Westbourne Grove
W11 (Notting Hill Gate Tube)

PHONE
0207 221 5218

HOURS
Mon.–Sat. 10:30 a.m.–5:30 p.m.

WEBSITE
www.galio.co.uk
$$–$$$

## 13 Galio Jewelers
*Fine Contemporary Jewelry*

Galio offers well-designed, fine contemporary jewelry, wedding and engagement rings, and watches in 18-karat gold and platinum. The store carries the works of selected designers, including Diana Porter, Sarah Jordan, Neissing, and Christian Bauer, some of whom design specifically for Galio. If you don't see your perfect bijou, the shop also offers a design service. The website shows a good selection of Galio's wares.

## 14 B&T Antiques

*Twentieth-Century Antique Furniture*

"People tell me I have very much my own look," says Bernadette Lewis. You spot it even before you enter her shop. She began collecting twentieth-century deco furniture decades ago and has been selling it from this location for twenty years. She's famous ("If that is the word," she says) in the trade for her mirrored French art-deco furniture from the '30s, '40s, and '50s, and reproduction art-deco mirrors that she designs and commissions.

Lewis's look includes unusual lighting, such as glass lamps, aluminum fixtures, and French industrial lights from the 1920s. Poke around downstairs to find metal furniture originally designed for the military and industry. The pieces, stripped of their gray paint, are fabulously designed and ready to fit into mixed decorating schemes.

ADDRESS
79–81 Ledbury Road
W11 (Ladbroke Grove or Notting Hill Gate Tube)

PHONE
0207 229 7001

HOURS
Mon.–Sat. 10:00 a.m.–6:00 p.m.
$$–$$$

## 15 Brora

*Cashmere*

ADDRESS
66 Ledbury Road
W11

(*See page 178 for full description.*)

## 16   Sean Arnold Sporting Antiques

*Sports Antiques and Memorabilia*

ADDRESS
1 Pembridge Villas
(corner of Westbourne Grove)
W2 (Notting Hill Gate Tube)

PHONE
0207 221 2267

HOURS
Mon.–Sat. 10:00 a.m.–6:00 p.m.
and by appointment
$–$$

This beautiful shop is brimming with antique sports equipment to tempt even armchair athletes and casual collectors. Cricket bats, polo mallets, oars from Cambridge boat crews, tennis rackets, leather rugby balls, golf balls, vintage luggage—items sell for as little as £16 for an old polo whip; £3 for a polo ball. There's a private sports museum open by appointment.

The shop is at the convergence of Pembridge Villas, Chepstow Place, and Westbourne Grove; the entrance is off Chepstow Road.

## 17   L Boutique

*Women's Clothing*

ADDRESS
28 Chepstow Corner, Chepstow Place
W2 (Notting Hill Gate Tube)

PHONE
0207 243 9190

HOURS
Tues.–Sat. 10:30 a.m.–6:00 p.m.

WEBSITE
www.thelboutique.com
$$–$$$

The company's motto is "irresistibly superfluous," an apt description of the beaded velvet coats, brocade jackets, satin trousers, beaded halters, and other finely wrought garments sold here. The clothing is handmade in one of four color "stories" each season so that pieces coordinate nicely and you get exactly the silhouette you want. You'll find Chinese silk brocade jackets from £350; silk velvet jackets from £350; coats from £595; devore scarves, £135.

## 18 Spa@NK

A day spa run by the beauty apothecary Space.NK (*see page 85*). Choose from a menu of massages, exfoliations, tanning, and waxing. An aromatherapy indulgence massage is £80 for ninety minutes.

ADDRESS
127–131 Westbourne Grove
W2 (Notting Hill Gate Tube)

PHONE
0207 727 8002

HOURS
Mon. 10:00 a.m.–7:00 p.m.;
Tues.–Thurs. 9:00 a.m.–9:00 p.m.;
Fri. 10:00 a.m.–7:00 p.m.;
Sat. 9:00 a.m.–7:00 p.m.;
Sun. 10:00 a.m.–5:00 p.m.

WEBSITE
www.spacenk.co.uk
$–$$

## 19 Special Photographers Company
*Fine Photography*

Photography collecting has not reached the pitch in England that it has in the States, and prices on fine photography are somewhat lower. The Special Photographers Company represents a wide range of photographers and styles from conceptual artists producing highly manipulated images to lyrical landscape photographers to shootists cranking out rock star candids. The company offers works by Wolfgang Suscitzky, Gary Woods, Bill Brandt, Milton Greene, Sheila Rock, Brassai, Tania Hirschberg, and many others. The website displays a good selection of the stock.

ADDRESS
236 Westbourne Park Road
W11 (Westbourne Park Tube)

PHONE
0207 221 3489

HOURS
Mon.–Fri. 10:00 a.m.–5:30 p.m.;
Sat. 11:00 a.m.–5:30 p.m.

WEBSITE
www.specialphotographers.com
$–$$

## 20 ScreenFace
*Theatrical Makeup and Supplies*

This shop is larger than the Covent Garden location (*see page 82*), which means more cosmetics, wigs, bruise kits, fake blood, temporary tattoos, body glitter, henna hand-paint kits, liquid latex, old-age makeup, and multicolored fake eyelashes. Was there anything else you needed?

ADDRESS
20 and 24 Powis Terrace
(off Westbourne Park Road)
W11 (Westbourne Park Tube)

PHONE
0207 221 8289

HOURS
Mon.–Sat. 9:00 a.m.–6:00 p.m.
$

# CULTURE ALONG THE WAY

ADDRESS
46 Ledbury Road

PHONE
0207 229 6187

HOURS
Mon.–Sat. 10:00 a.m.–6:00 p.m.

WEBSITE
www.pissarro.net

## Stern Pissarro Gallery

Painter Camille Pissarro was the patriarch of an especially large and talented family. The Stern Pissarro Gallery features works in many media by four generations of the artistic Pissarros, some still producing art. The gallery is a pleasant stop for admiring the work of this dynasty. You can usually expect an exhibition focusing on a particular topic or technique.

Downstairs is a collection of nineteenth-century paintings by other artists, priced attractively (most below £5,000) for the casual buyer. The website is very thorough, with plenty of images and information, including exhibitions.

# WHERE TO EAT

ADDRESS
39 Chepstow Place
W2 (Notting Hill Gate Tube)

PHONE
0207 792 5501

## Assaggi

This tiny, elegant second-floor dining room over a bar has been a big success by employing a simple formula: Choose the finest ingredients and handle them lightly. The menu confines itself to ten starters, several salads, and a half-dozen main courses, so you'd think choosing would be easy. It's not, because everything sounds, and is, wonderful. Each ingredient is given the treatment that best showcases it—pecorino is thinly sliced before being fried and settled on a bed of arugula with just a drizzle of fine-quality olive oil. Fish is selected for its freshness; milk-fed lamb is brought to your table before being carved. Homemade bread, best-quality olive oil, fine Parmesan, and absolutely fresh ingredients make for excellent, if somewhat expensive, dining.

Expect dinner to cost around £40 per person. The interesting wine list offers some bargains (from £13.95) and some extravagances (up to £60) as well as grappas and digestifs. As Assaggi is very popular and has only about ten tables, evening reservations can be a challenge, but the staff works hard to be accommodating. Lunch and weekday dinners are a surer thing. The entrance is on the side of the building. Walk into the passage to the left of the building and the door is on the right.

## Bed Bar

A Moroccan-themed bar of purple velvet décor, draped chandeliers, incense, and big mattress-like cushions for sitting or lying (hence the name). If you were a certain type of twenty- or thirty-something, this place could meet all your drinking, dining, and entertainment needs. Breakfast is served every day. Sundays bring a traditional Sunday roast. North African menu the rest of the time. About a hundred vodkas and rums are offered, along with a DJ from Thursday to Sunday—you'd never have to leave. Nighttime is probably kinder to the interior—during the day it looks a little worn, as if there had been a big party the night before. There probably was. Get a look at the interior and the schedule on the website.

ADDRESS
310 Portobello Road
W10

PHONE
0208 969 4500

WEBSITE
www.styleinthecity.co.uk

## The Cow

The Cow and its rival across the street, the Westbourne, are what Brits call "gastropubs," friendly local joints serving upscale food at reasonable prices while maintaining a pub atmosphere. Seafood is the Cow's forte: The Cow Special is six rock oysters and a pint of Guinness (£9). Downstairs at the bar or at one of a handful of tables, get a lunch of monkfish with cockles and samphire (£13.50), or peppered sirloin with watercress salad (£12). The upstairs dining room opens at 7:00 p.m., offering a starter of grilled squid with chipotle salsa (£8.50), homemade pasta with ricotta and rocket (£13), and a veal T-bone (£17). A couple of dozen bottles make up the wine list, including fifteen by the glass. You'll probably need a reservation for the dining room.

ADDRESS
89 Westbourne Park Road
W2

PHONE
0207 221 5400
(Reservations: 0207 221 0021)

If you can't get in the Cow, try the Westbourne across the street for similarly good food.

## Sausage & Mash Café

ADDRESS
268 Portobello Road
W10
PHONE
0208 968 8898
HOURS
Mon.–Sat. 11:00 a.m.–11:00 p.m.;
Sun. 11:00 a.m.–10:30 p.m.

Don't let the sign, S&M Café, or its under-the-bridge location beneath the Westway put you off this cheap-and-cheerful place. Inside, the décor is nicely minimal and modern, and you'll be rewarded with a good, very inexpensive meal.

The system is straightforward: Choose a sausage from the ten daily offerings. Choose a style or flavor of mash (mashed potato), then choose a gravy. They put together a mountainous plateful of it for you. You tuck in.

But this is no greasy spoon: The sausages are high-quality, in modern flavor combinations like lamb and mint, chicken and leek, and pork and chili, as well as vegetarian options. Gravies include red onion, thyme and Madeira, or other poshed-up combinations.

They have a selection of wine and beer.

## Clarke's

ADDRESS
124 Kensington Church Street
W8 (Notting Hill Gate Tube)

California-inspired cuisine. (*See page 122.*)

## & Clarke

ADDRESS
122 Kensington Church Street
(Notting Hill Gate Tube)
PHONE
0207 229 2190

Bakery and deli. (*See page 122.*)

## The Churchill Arms

ADDRESS
119 Kensington Church Street
(Notting Hill Gate Tube or
Kensington High Street Tube)
PHONE
0207 792 1246

English pub in front; Thai restaurant in back. (*See page 123.*)

# INDEX

---